Spirituality of the Handmaid

For
Stephen Casey
and
Andrew Sherman—

Called from the womb

My speaking is motivated by poverty and want, rather than by riches and abundance. In the end this negative motivation may be as good as any. In the kingdom of God there are no possessors—only beggars. Even the elementary rule of human prudence does not apply: Of that which we know not we must remain silent. Of God no one "knows" and so it must be desire rather than possession that urges us to speak.

—Rene Dupré
The Deeper Life

Spirituality of the Handmaid

A Model for Contemporary Seekers

Kerry Walters

PAULIST PRESS
New York / Mahwah, N.J.

The Publisher gratefully acknowledges use of the following: Excerpt from *The Collected Works of Edith Stein: The Hidden Life,* translated by Waltraut Stein, Ph.D.: Copyright 1992 by Washington Province of Discalced Carmelites. Used by permission of ICS Publications; 2131 Lincoln Road, N.E.; Washington, D.C. 20002 USA. Excerpts from *Collected Poems* by Wallace Stevens: Copyright 1942 by Wallace Stevens. Reprinted by permission of Alfred A. Knopf and Faber & Faber, London. Excerpt from "Ash Wednesday" from *The Complete Poems and Plays 1909–1950,* copyright 1930 and renewed 1958 by T. S. Eliot. Reprinted by permission of Harcourt Brace and Company and Faber and Faber, London. Excerpt from *White Pine: Poems and Prose Poems* by Mary Oliver: Copyright by Mary Oliver. Published by Harcourt Brace and Company.

Illustrations by Brother Michael O'Neill McGrath

Cover design by Moe Berman

Interior design by Millennium Wordpress

Library of Congress Cataloging-in-Publication Data

Walters, Kerry S.
  Spirituality of the handmaid : a model for contemporary seekers / by Kerry Walters.
    p.   cm.
  Includes bibliographical references.
  ISBN 0-8091-3851-4 (alk. paper)
  1. Spirituality—Catholic Church. 2. Mary, Blessed Virgin, Saint—Apparitions and miracles—Bosnia and Herzegovina—Medjugorje. I. Title.
    BX2350.65.W35   1999
248.4'82—dc21   98-32267
                                                                      CIP

Published by Paulist Press
997 Macarthur Boulevard
Mahwah, New Jersey 07430

www.paulistpress.com

Printed and bound in the
United States of America

Contents

Contents

Chapter Three: Conversion 101

Two Brothers...Scriptural Lessons...Reward-Love...Turning...Imitatio Christi

Notes 140

Acknowledgments

I've been privileged while writing this book to become indebted to a number of people:

To my wife Kim, who believed in the project; to Jonah, who patiently endured his dad's sometimes tiresome preoccupation with book writing; to Lisa Portmess, Chan Coulter, Karmen MacKendrick, Lou Hammann, and Hanno Bulhof for their true and constant fellowship; to Ed and Cynthia Johnson for their goodwill and generosity; to Mother Lynn Carter-Edmands and Father Mark McCullough for their inspiration and wisdom; to Michael O'Neill McGrath, O.S.F.S., whose drawings of Mary took away my breath as soon as I laid eyes on them; and to my editor Kathleen Walsh, who shepherded the manuscript with humor, sensitivity, enthusiasm, and expertise. All authors should be so lucky!

The book is dedicated to two men who have taught me more than they'll ever know, much less take credit for. Stephen Casey and Andrew Sherman are genuine Godbearers. I've merely written about the Handmaid's way, but they live it. Stephen and Andrew, I thank God for you both.

Introduction

Godbearing

You will conceive in your womb....
Luke 1:31

I am your mother and therefore I want to lead all of you to perfect holiness.
Medjugorje
25 May 1987

Truly, truly, I say to you, unless one is born anew, he cannot see the kingdom of God.
John 3:3

Fire on the Mountain, Fire in the Heart

Hidden away in the high country of Bosnia-Herzegovina is a tiny village of some four hundred families. It's called Medjugorje, which means "between the mountains." The hamlet, neatly tucked as it is between Mount Podbrdo and Mount Krizevac, is well named.

Until recently the people of Medjugorje lived in relative anonymity. Their village was so insignificant that its existence was overlooked by most cartographers. But all this changed in the early summer of 1981. On June 24 of that year, the feast day of St. John the Baptist, two of the village's teenage girls glanced up at Mount Podbrdo. It was early twilight. An uncanny light shimmered around the small mountain's summit, and afloat in the midst of it was a beautiful woman holding an infant. She called to the girls, who fled in terror. But they were also strangely attracted by what they'd seen, and in spite of their fear returned later that night with several of their friends. The mountain was still suffused with light, and the lady was still there. She identified herself as the Virgin Mary, the Blessed Mother of God.

Word of what the girls saw spread quickly among the villagers. Some (including, initially, Father Jozo, the local priest) were skeptical, while others were convinced that the apparition was genuine. But everyone was curious. The next evening, June 25, a large crowd assembled to gaze upon the mountain. At approximately 6:40 great flashes of light started bouncing off Podbrdo onto nearby Mount Krizevac. The flashes were so intense that some watching them feared the hills would melt. Suddenly six children in the crowd, the two teenagers from the night before and four others, fell to their knees in ecstasy. Each experienced a vision of Mary, her arms extended, beckoning to them. The rest of the crowd saw only the lights, but these six children, now collectively known as the "visionaries," saw and heard the Virgin.[1]

The fire on Mount Podbrdo (since renamed Apparition Hill) which first appeared on that summer night over fifteen years ago is still burning, and it has catapulted the name *Medjugorje* into international prominence. To this day the apparitions of the Virgin Mary continue. Millions of pilgrims have journeyed to Medjugorje to worship at Mount Podbrdo and speak to the visionaries. Miraculous physical cures have been reported, holy medals have supposedly changed color, and thousands claim to have witnessed the uncanny fire on the mountain as well as a solar miracle in which the sun seems a huge fireball whose spinning brilliance does not blind the naked eye. In May 1986 a Vatican-appointed commission was authorized to begin an official investigation of the apparitions and miracles.

Since March 1984 the Blessed Mother has sent a monthly message to the world through the visionary children. These messages, as recorded, are terse and remarkably consistent. They call upon the peoples of the earth to fast, to pray, and to convert. They appear not to be directed exclusively to Christian believers, but to adherents of all faiths: as one of the visionaries reported, "The Madonna said that religions are separated in the earth, but the people of all religions are accepted by her Son."[2]

Dozens of books have been written about the events at Medjugorje.[3] All of them have enthusiastically focused either exclusively or primarily on the supernatural character of the apparitions and miracles, and the popular press has followed their lead. This is understandable because the human imagination has always been riveted by such signs and wonders (cf. Mt 12:38–39, Mk 8:12, 1 Cor 1:22). But serious reflection on the deeper spiritual meaning of Mary's message to the world is all too often buried under the hundreds of pages recording anecdotes of cures, flashing lights, and solar fireballs. This is unfortunate because, if the Blessed Mother is indeed communicating to the Medjugorje visionaries, it is her message, not the allegedly supernatural events associated with it, that is central. The miracle of the sun and the flashing mountain lights could one day be explained away as hallucinations or atmospheric phenomena, physical cures as temporary hysteria, and color changes in holy medals as mere oxidation. But none of these, should they occur, would affect the depth or richness of the spiritual message relayed to us through the visionary children. The more important fire from Medjugorje is not found on mountain tops, but in the hearts of those who have heard and responded to Mary's call for renewal through fasting, prayer, and conversion.

This book is an exploration of the great spiritual vision that lies at the heart of the Virgin's tripartite message, a vision I call "Handmaid spirituality" after Mary's designation of herself, recorded in Luke's Gospel, as the "handmaid of the Lord." In the chapters that follow I show how Mary's Medjugorje call for fasting, prayer, and conversion offers to those of us who hear it a grace-filled way of deepening our lived relationship with God. In this introduction I wish to set the stage for those chapters by sketching in broad outline the signature characteristics and aims of Handmaid spirituality. But in order to do that, some preliminary remarks about what I mean by the word *spirituality* are in order.

Understanding Spirituality

There are few words in the religious lexicon more amorphous than *spirituality*. Its meaning has been so broadened by popular usage that it has almost become a tag word for anything that smacks of piety or inwardness or rectitude. The upshot is that our relation to the word *spirituality* frequently parallels St. Augustine's perplexity over the word *time*. In his *Confessions* he tells us that he knows perfectly well what *time* means until someone asks him to define it; then, he laments, he's at a loss.[4] Similarly, many of us tend to throw the word *spirituality* around in our conversation with great facility. But if called to explain what we mean by it, we most likely would find it difficult to do so.

A clearer understanding of spirituality is possible if we

reflect on the meaning of its root word, *spirit.* Originally, in Hebrew *(ruach)* as well as Greek *(pneuma)*—and also, it seems, in Latin, Sanskrit, and English—the word suggested an image rather than a theological concept. That image is of a breeze or breath that stirs the air and vitalizes whatever it touches. In Genesis (1:2), for example, the act of divine creation is inaugurated by the spirit or *ruach* of God blowing through the formless void and imparting structure and inner meaning to it. Parallel to the original creative act described in Genesis, God's spirit *(pneuma)* at Pentecost sweeps around and through Jesus' disciples "like the blowing of a violent wind...from heaven," breathing life into their interior formless voids (Acts 2:1–4).

In both of these scriptural stories the image of a vitalizing breath or breeze symbolizes the conviction that there is a God-initiated creativity at work in the universe. It infuses a deep meaning into the very fabric of existence that both undergirds and transcends the visible and material objects presented to our senses. It is neither passive nor totally separated from that which it indwells. Instead, it is an active presence in the midst of the world, the vivifying and ongoing participation of God in his creation. As such, *pneuma, ruach*—spirit—is "that manner of the Divine Being in which he comes closest, dwells with us, acts upon us."[5]

We are now in a better position to understand the meaning of *spirituality.* It is a generic word denoting that process whereby humans strive to open themselves to the divine spirit creatively indwelling them and the rest of the world. We are tabernacles of the spirit, participants (whether we acknowledge it or not) in the sacred. This is our essential identity. Our task is to realize, cooperate with, and grow into the spirit that defines us. In Pauline terms, we are called to shuck off our egos, to "crucify the flesh with its passions and desires" (Gal 5:24), renew our inmost being (Eph 4:23), and put on Christ. The lifelong endeavor to become more abundant in Christ by inviting the divine wind to blow through one's soul is what we call *spirituality,* and its fruits, as Paul assures us, are "love, joy, peace, patience, kindness, goodness, faithfulness, gentleness, self-control" (Gal 5:22–23).

Writers on the spiritual life have appealed over the centuries to any number of metaphors to reexpress Paul's insight that the essence of Christ-growth is the nurturing of the indwelling spirit. Some two centuries after Paul, for example, Origen declared that each of us carries deep within a "well of living water." It is an interior spring, Origen says, because the kingdom of God is found in our hearts. Our task is to cooperate with the divine spirit by removing the clay from our souls so that the spring may flow freely. Abruptly switching metaphors but still focusing on interiority, Origen continues:

> It was not outside but in her house that the woman who had lost her silver coin found it again (Luke 15:8). She had lighted the lamp and swept out the house, and it was there that she found her silver coin. For your part, if you light your "lamp," if you make use of the illumination of the Holy Spirit, if you "see light in his light," you will find the silver coin in you....It could not be seen in you as long as your house was dirty, full of refuse and rubbish....[But] the buried image of God remains in you always.[6]

In the sixth century the pseudonymous mystic Dionysius the Areopagite also tried to capture the Pauline insight. "It may be true," he wrote, "that the divine principle is present in every being, but not every being is present in him." The Aeropagite goes on to liken the process of making contact with (or becoming "present in") the indwelling *pneuma* to a shipwrecked sailor's strategy for reaching haven. "If we were on a ship, and to rescue us ropes attached to a rock were thrown to us, obviously we should not draw the rock any nearer to ourselves, but we would pull ourselves and our ship nearer to the rock." Analogously, he concludes, the spiritual life consists not in "drawing to ourselves that Power that is everywhere and nowhere, but by putting ourselves in his hands and uniting ourselves to him."[7]

The aim of the spiritual life, so picturesquely expressed by these and other authors, is an increasingly committed plumbing of the depths of the living wellspring that fructifies our interior landscape and transforms our behavior in the world. But there is no single prescribed method of clearing away the "refuse and rubbish" we've allowed to clog it. One of the most obvious and exhilarating facts about the divine creation is its complexity and diversity. The spirit indwells all humans, but each person is a unique nexus of temperament, aptitude, and needs. The Church, inspired, we may presume, by the Holy Spirit, has recognized this diversity for some two millennia, and a number of spiritualities suited to fit differences in personality has evolved as a consequence. All draw upon scripture and tradition as ultimate inspirations, and thus there is a clear family resemblance among them. But each also employs characteristic techniques and modes of expression that distinguish it from the others. Some, for example, emphasize the language and lifestyle of contemplative prayer; others, charismatic celebration. Some accentuate ascetic withdrawal and others works of mercy in the midst of the world. The Father's house has many rooms. Regardless of the diverse paths laid out by different Christian spiritual traditions, however, they all aim at the same goal: to nurture the God-seed within each human heart so that it may reach fruition and lead the devotee to fulfillment in Christ.

Theotokoi All

The characteristic signature of Handmaid spirituality—that vision of growing-into-Christ suggested by the Medjugorje messages, scriptural accounts of Mary, and the Church's long tradition of Marian devotion—is expressed in the language of conception, birth, and maternity. Mary is the *Theotokos,* the Godbearer, Mother of the Christ. She willingly received within herself the Godseed from which grew the incarnated Word. She lovingly nurtured that seed, feeding it with her own vitality, celebrating its life, allowing it to develop until it was ready to blossom forth. She cooperated with the spirit in its act of supreme creation, and in the process was herself made anew and drawn closer to God. In birthing God she helped birth herself. She also birthed, as scripture suggests (cf. Jn 19:26–27), all who have come after her. Each of us is her daughter or son. She is the spiritual mother of us all.

Handmaid spirituality takes Mary's living example as its inspiration, inviting us to emulate her archetypal response to God's call. Like her, we are *Theotokoi.* The spirit of God dwells in us and we are summoned, under Mary's guidance, to nurture that divine seed with love and sacrifice and celebration. As Meister Eckhart preached in the fourteenth century, the nativity takes place again and again in the hearts of all believers; Christmas is always.[8] Mary's example reminds us that we are born to be agents of the continuing Incarnation so that our souls, like hers, may magnify the Lord (Lk 1:46).

The Medjugorje messages time and again emphasize the maternal nature of Mary's spirituality, both in the way that she promises to guide us toward God with motherly devotion and compassion, and in the way she encourages us to follow her example by allowing God to gestate in our own souls. She invites us to "press tight" against her "motherly heart" so that she may "shepherd" us toward spiritual maturity.[9] Her wish is to "bear" us "unto holiness" as she "bore Jesus in [her] womb."[10] Like all good mothers she realizes that children are frequently headstrong and will insist on going their own way. But she assures us that she is a loving parent who "forgive[s] easily" and "rejoice[s] for every child who comes back."[11] Her motivation is motherly love, and she wishes to impart that great love to those of us who are her children: "Be aware, my beloved, that I am your mother and that I have come to the earth to teach you how to listen out of love, how to pray out of love."[12] In instructing us in the way of love, she helps us realize God within us and leads us closer to the "Tabor experience"[13] of spiritual birth.

A Spiritual Mosaic

Handmaid spirituality, then, calls for a birthing in and of our souls, for which Mary's own bearing of Christ is the eternal exemplar. This emphasis on "the birth of the little Jesus...in [our] daily lives" is the distinctive hallmark of her spirituality.[14] Its ultimate goal, as she metaphorically tells us, is to "make a very beautiful mosaic" of our hearts so that she "might be able to present each one of [us] to God like the original image."[15]

Mary's metaphor of a heart mosaic is especially intriguing. The word *mosaic,* derived from *muses,* the nine goddesses who in Greek mythology represented artistic creativity, refers of course to any picture or design made by inlaying thousands of pieces of colored stone or glass side by side in mortar. The word functions grammatically as either verb or noun, suggesting both a creative act lovingly undertaken by the artist as well as the end product of her labor. Like all acts of genuine creativity, a mosaic design arises as inspiration from deep within the artist's psyche and is gradually, patiently, brought to fruition by dedicated persistence and skill. In working on a mosaic, the artist inevitably discovers dimensions to it that weren't readily apparent to her at its inception. When completed, the mosaic is a thing of beautiful complexity whose revelatory power frequently startles and awes even the artist herself.[16]

The actual piecing together of a mosaic usually proceeds from the center outwards. The artist initially focuses on the compositional nucleus of the design she has imagined, first inlaying its foundational tiles and then extending the center's radius, tile by tile, until the work is brought to completion. The initial tile is the keystone that determines the piece's overall coherency.

Structurally, the finished mosaic may be said to be a harmonious composite of tensions. The picture or design that the artist wishes to create in the mosaic only emerges because she juxtaposes tiles of various colors next to one another. The image that her creative activity expresses, then, is born from contrast: reds next to blues, whites side by side with blacks, and so on. When viewed close-up, the contrast between the contiguously laid tiles often appears discordant and jumbled. But if one steps back to gain a perspective on the whole, the eye is presented with a wondrously complex pattern whose harmony emerges precisely because of its underlying tension.

This image of a mosaic is a metaphor for the process of spiritual birthing which is the goal of the Handmaid's way. Just as the pattern of a physical mosaic is born from artistic inspiration, so the spiritual renewal represented by the symbol of a heart mosaic originates in the interior quickening brought about by the divine *pneuma*. The Godseed that hitherto has lain dormant in the soul stirs, exciting an interior response and subsequent course of development whose ultimate purpose is often intuited only dimly by the Godbearer. As the gestation process unfolds, the individual is inevitably startled at the unforeseen turns it takes and the revelations it discloses. She comes to realize that the incredible richness and beauty toward which she is headed and which she but roughly grasped at the beginning of the process far surpasses anything she could have anticipated.

This spiritual birthing, moreover, proceeds from the inside out. The Godseed that has quickened within the individual's heart serves as the spiritual center of gravity that grounds and makes sense of the future course of her growth in God. The interior renewal expands until it transfigures her, eventually extending its radius to restructure her intellect, her volition, and her behavior into a beautiful unity with God's will. As Pseudo-Macarius puts it, "...then the soul and the Lord are one spiritually, they form one life, one heart."[17]

But the spiritual harmony achieved in the growth of the heart mosaic, like the compositional harmony of a mosaic of stone or glass, is born from tension. As noted earlier, a necessary condition for the emergence of a physical mosaic is that the contrast between its constitutive tiles gives rise to a whole that incorporates and transcends the contrast. Analogously, a necessary condition for the birth of a heart mosaic is that the individual's predictably ambivalent and often contradictory responses to the spirit stirring within her do likewise. Spiritual birthing, like artistic creation, is not an easy process, and the person in whom Godseed has quickened is apt to experience both surrender and resistance, anticipation and anxiety, joy and pain. This is an inevitable feature of spiritual mothering, and it is also the necessary condition for spiritual birth. As Meister Eckhart observed of spiritual birthing, "...the shell must be cracked apart if what is in it is to come out, for if you want the kernel you must break the shell."[18] But Jesus promised (Jn 16:21) that harmonious and joyful growth would follow the initially painful shell cracking: "When a woman is in travail she has sorrow, because her hour has come; but when she is delivered of the child, she no longer remembers the anguish, for joy that a child is born into the world."

Labor Pains

The spiritual tensions that characterize our own Godbearing are reflections of those experienced by Mary in hers. Humans naturally wish to avoid or anesthetize discomfort, but Handmaid spirituality teaches us that the spiritual pain that accompanies Godbearing must be embraced just as fully as its promise. Both are necessary moments in the soul's renewal: the labor pains of birthing as well as the sense of joyful fulfillment that follows. They are the contrasting tiles that form the heart mosaic.

This pattern of pain and promise characteristic of Godbearing is central to Handmaid spirituality and will be discussed at some length in the chapters that follow. For now let me provide two illustrations of it, both taken from Luke's account of the Annunciation. These stories are pivotal. They serve as archetypal models of spiritual quickening, and they remind us that the ultimate meaningfulness of our own labor pains is guaranteed by Mary's experience.

The first story from Luke is this: When the angel Gabriel hailed Mary, her initial reaction was panic. Luke (1:29) laconically records that she was "greatly troubled" at the angel's appearance and bewildered by his greeting. Greatly troubled indeed! When the breath of God touches an individual busily engaged in the process of everyday life, the temple veil that separates the sacred from the profane is rent asunder and can never be mended. Mary, like any mortal, must have been terrified by the sudden inrush of spirit, paralyzed with the awful realization that the earth and heavens had so uncannily moved.

But side by side with her dread at the prospect of the life-changing event overtaking her, Mary also experienced a piercing joy, the joy of a soon-to-be mother who feels the quickening of life beneath her breast. The pain of anxiety danced with exultation, and from the midst of both she ecstatically shouted out a hymn of thanksgiving for the fearful and wondrous gift: "My soul magnifies the Lord, and my spirit rejoices in God my Savior!" (Lk 1:46–47). Conflicting responses, contrasting tiles. On the one hand, the first stirring of Godseed brings the searing realization that one's life has turned an unexpected corner and that things will never be what they were. On the other hand, the spiritual quickening brings an exhilaration atremble with anticipation that a great mystery, laden with promise and fulfillment, beckons. Both the fear and the anticipation are necessary moments in the creation of a heart mosaic. Both must be embraced.

Here's the second story: Luke also tells us that Gabriel sought to reassure the anxious young woman by offering her the glad tidings that she had been chosen to bear the Messiah. But Mary initially refused to accept this. "How could this possibly be?" she balked. "I've known no husband" (Lk 1:34). Embedded in Mary's objection is an emphatic *no!* It's not difficult to imagine what must have been coursing through her mind: *This is my life! I haven't chosen this! I don't want this! Leave me alone! I'm to marry Joseph and be the mother of his children! I want a normal life!* It is a difficult thing to see one's cardhouse of fond hopes and careful plans for the future toppled by the breath of God. The will asserts itself, the ego rebels against the loss of self-direction. But Gabriel persisted. The power of God has overshadowed you, he told Mary. It's no good straining against the harness. Just trust God; nothing is impossible with him (Lk 1:35, 37). And from Mary's initial rebellion emerged the realization that the future so abruptly handed her was her destiny. It is what she was created for, and submission to it was the necessary condition for discovering genuine freedom. She bowed her head and replied: "Behold, I am the handmaid of the Lord; let it be to me according to your word" (Lk 1:38). Willful rebellion and trusting submission: two more contrasting tiles in the heart mosaic, two additional moments in the labor pain of Godbearing that show us what it means to walk in and with the spirit.

The Original Image

Handmaid spirituality teaches us how to anticipate and respond to the various labor pains of Godbearing. As we've seen, an embrace of the pain as well as the promise allows for the blossoming of the divine spirit within us, leading ultimately to the rebirth in Christ symbolized by Mary's image of a heart mosaic. But there's one more aspect of this rebirth that needs to be considered. Mary tells us that the piecing together of a heart mosaic restores us to our "original image." What does this mean?

Pre-Christian philosophers such as Aristotle and Plotinus believed that every created thing is directed toward an ultimate end, or *telos,* that is proper to it by virtue of the sort of thing it is.[19] The proper end of an acorn, for example, is to grow into an oak. This is what an acorn is meant to do, and its purpose or reason for existing is realized when that end is achieved. An acorn may, of course, serve other purposes. It can wind up as winter food for a squirrel or be glued to a sheet of construction paper by an artistic preschooler. But neither of these uses is proper to what an acorn is, and consequently

— 14 —

neither fulfills its *telos.* Instead, each is a thwarting of its ultimate end.

Now, to be a human is likewise to be a created thing. Consequently, there must be a purpose or *telos* proper to humans, and its actualization results in a person's attainment of the end for which he or she was created. Conversely, the thwarting of that end prevents an individual from reaching fulfillment. Saints Augustine and Thomas Aquinas, picking up where their Greek predecessors left off, argued that the ultimate end toward which all humans are directed is also their source: God. Augustine's entire *Confessions,* as he points out in the book's opening paragraph, is an attempt to demonstrate that we are made for God and are restless until we realize our destination. Thomas likewise argues that humans, made in the image of God, are unfulfilled both psychologically and metaphysically until we become aware of our true nature and strive to live up to it.[20]

Augustine and Thomas concur, then, that to be a human is to be stamped in God's likeness—a claim that is the philosophical expression of Handmaid spirituality's signature insight that Godseed indwells each of us—and that our well-being ultimately depends on growing into that likeness. But obviously most of us do not act in accordance with who we are. As we walk along life's path we bury the Godseed under layers of self-will, greed, and worldly distractions, wandering farther and farther away from where we are meant to go. The Blessed Mother's example calls us to rediscover who we really are and thereby to remember our proper end—a living in and through and with our divine source. By following the Handmaid's way we fulfill our telos and are reborn into our original image. We relinquish our hearts of stone and receive hearts of flesh, and when we do that, as St. Benedict declares, we "run the ways of God's commandments in an ineffable sweetness of love."[21]

In the Zen Buddhist tradition, students are given spiritual riddles called *"koans"* to meditate on. One of the most famous *koans* is: "What did your face look like before you were born?" Handmaid spirituality aims to help Christians uncover and live the answer to that question.

Medjugorje's Message Today

The messages from Medjugorje are unequivocal: the process of Godbearing, the construction of a heart mosaic, the recovery of our original image, are attained through fasting, prayer, and conversion. These three are interlocking moments, valid yesterday, today, and tomorrow, in the soul's discovery and celebration of the spirit that indwells it. But every generation has the responsibility of interpreting and communicating this insight in its own words and idiom. This is not to say that the metaphors and techniques of spiritual traditions from bygone ages have nothing to teach us, but only that the eternal truths expressed in Mary's tripartite message must also be filtered through late twentieth-century language if they are to speak to contemporary hearts and minds. When the Holy Spirit communicated through the apostles at Pentecost, it deigned to express its eternal message in a language understandable to each of the assembled hearers. That divine accommodation to the ears and minds of the faithful teaches us a valuable lesson: God speaks, but in his wisdom makes use of the idiom to which we're accustomed. Interpreters of God's word should follow the divine lead.

I've tried to take that lesson to heart in this book by walking the narrow path, by honoring the timeless validity of Handmaid spirituality's call for fasting, prayer, and conversion while simultaneously exploring and interpreting the message in language that speaks to today's Christian. Mary invites us to be *Theotokoi* and thereby realize our original and eternal image; but temporal and contextual creatures that we are, we can only do so in the language and thoughts of our own time and place.

Chapter 1 explores the meaning for today's Christian of Mary's call to *fasting.* As we'll see, all of us naturally yearn for an encounter with the indwelling spirit, but too often we try to satiate this deep-seated soul-hunger by gorging on worldly substitutes instead of the true object of our desire. Fasting is the spiritual purgative that allows us to wean ourselves from our distracting addiction to junk food and thereby prepare ourselves for an encounter with the true meaning of our hunger. It cleanses the spiritual palate and increases our sensitivity to the Godseed that indwells us. Fasting is not in itself a putting-on-of-Christ so much as a discipline for becoming receptive to our yearning for Christ.

After we've liberated ourselves from our misguided gorging through an embrace of soul-hunger, we are ready to listen to the indwelling Godseed. This listening, done in reverence and hope and love, is the essence of *prayer,* explored in chapter 2. Just as gorging is the obstacle that stands in the way of recognizing the true nature of soul-hunger, so word-bewitchment is the chief enemy of genuine prayer. The quickening of Godseed is not brought about through formulaic recitations of worded prayers or frenetic verbal supplications. Instead, we become Godbearers when we nurture our relationship with the indwelling spirit through the cultivation of silence. Prayer is ultimately not something we *do* so much as what we *become* in the process of collaborating in the birthing of Christ within our hearts.

If fasting is a spiritual medicinal that prepares us to be

Godbearers, and prayer is the quickening and gestation of the Godseed within, *conversion* is the spiritual stage in which we birth the indwelling spirit and in so doing are ourselves born anew. As we'll see in chapter 3, the converted person, returned to her original image, is so unified with the indwelling spirit that her entire life is an oblation offered up in love and gratitude. Handmaid spirituality, no less than all other spiritual traditions, recognizes that any putative conversion that fails to lead to an external *imitatio Christi* as well as an interior turning is in fact no conversion at all. The essence of this imitation is self-emptying love. In chapter 3 we'll explore the nature and challenge of living as *Theotokoi* by taking a look at what it means to live this love and how to avoid the perversion that blocks genuine conversion.

Two final words are necessary. Although this book explores fasting, prayer, and conversion in a sequential order, and although it's certainly the case that they are successive moments that all of us who follow the Handmaid's way go through in our efforts to become *Theotokoi,* I do not want to give the impression that they are rigidly blocked-out stages in the soul's progression toward God. While it's true that fasting prepares the way for prayer and conversion, it's also the case that the prayerful urge to harken to God's will is present, even if only implicitly, in our attempts at fasting. Similarly, fasting is an ongoing discipline that necessarily accompanies both prayer and conversion. Perhaps the most accurate description of the interaction among purging, listening, and witnessing is that the higher moments fully incorporate the lower ones—conversion includes prayer and fasting, prayer includes fasting—but with the understanding that prayer and conversion are also nascent in the initial discipline of fasting. Handmaid spirituality's three foundations, then, are dynamic rather than static. They inevitably interpenetrate one another to such an extent that it is misleading to draw clear-cut boundaries between them. They are as intimately connected to and dependent upon one another as are the tiles of a mosaic.

Secondly, it should always be kept in mind that the act of Godbirthing, which is Handmaid spirituality's goal, is ultimately initiated by God. We are called to be cocreators through the disciplines of fasting, prayer, and conversion, but our role is ever that of junior partner. God's loving initiative in his invitation to Mary is recapitulated in each of us: He beckons and we follow. If fasting, prayer, and conversion are strategies for constructing the metaphorical heart mosaic, we must never forget that the original moment of inspiration, as well as the glue that holds the tiles together, is divine grace.

Chapter One

Fasting

He has filled the hungry with good things,
and the rich He has sent away empty.

Luke 1:53

Love God above all else in this time
when, due to the spirit of consumerism, one
forgets what it means to love and to cherish
true values.

Medjugorje
25 February 1996

Blessed are those who hunger....

Matthew 5:6

"Fast before the Lord"

The Godbearing to which Handmaid spirituality invites us is ultimately initiated and guided by divine grace. But as we saw in the introduction, we are called to cooperate in the process. Our task is to nurture the soil of our hearts so that the Godseed planted there quickens and comes to fruition. The first step in this spiritual gestation is a clearing away of brambles and flint so that the crop may grow and the promised harvest be reaped. This is done through the spiritual discipline of fasting.

The Virgin's Medjugorje messages are clear about the importance of fasting. Mary calls us to "fast strictly," not because doing so is a good in and of itself, but because it is a necessary condition for the growth into God which is our destiny.[1] She warns that we "are preoccupied about material things and in the material [we] lose everything God wants to give [us]"[2] The heart mosaic can only be constructed if we first prepare ourselves through "penance and fasting" and "renounce all the things to which [we] are attached" and which stand in the way of our spiritual development.[3] Fasting, then, is the regimen by which we cleanse ourselves of those impurities that pollute us spiritually and render us barren, so that, as St. Ambrose said, our spirits may be nourished.[4] The fourth-century desert father Evagrios Pontikos summed it up well. "Fast before the Lord according to your strength," he advised, "for to do this will purge you of your iniquities and sins; it exalts the soul, sanctifies the mind, drives away the demons, and prepares you for God's presence."[5]

This chapter explores the importance of fasting for the divine birthing that is the aim of Handmaid spirituality. As we'll see, the soul-hunger for God that it seeks to awaken and cultivate is in direct conflict with the worldly gorging the Medjugorje messages warn against. A glutton can gorge on religion and the ego as well as material commodities, and we'll discover that a genuine fasting before the Lord demands the renunciation of shallow pieties and "egolatry" as much as detachment from material addictions. But this doesn't mean that fasting is a relentlessly somber nay-saying to life. On the contrary, it is an embrace of our fundamental soul-hunger that brings great rejoicing to the individual who accepts its discipline. Pain and joy, renunciation and yea-saying: two sets of contrasting tiles that in fact are quite inseparable in the creation of a heart mosaic.

Trace Memories

Americans are gluttons, and genuine fasting doesn't come easily to us. We live in a consumer society that encourages us to belly up to an enticing smorgasbord of treats. We ravenously devour commodities, services, and entertainments, and petulantly complain if the foods we crave aren't immediately available. We also frenetically feed on people, glut ourselves on work, and avidly gobble up opportunities for social recognition. Our maws are enormous. We want larger and larger wedges of the pie and spend much of our time and energy conniving ways to push closer to the feeding trough.

Paradoxically, however, we are also a people obsessed with dieting. We periodically endure the latest regimen that promises a relatively painless shedding of extra pounds, and we spend millions of dollars each year to buy exercise equipment or memberships at gyms and health spas. (One of the more striking signs of our spiritual confusion is that we indulge in gluttony even when we try to purge ourselves of its effects.) We periodically recognize that our consumerist overeating is pernicious and solemnly pledge to adopt simpler lifestyles in order to get back in touch with what's "really important." We throw away the cigarettes, lock the booze cabinet, limit ourselves to two cups of coffee a day, unplug the television set, vow not to bring our work home with us, and resolve to spend more time with the kids. But our resolutions are usually short-lived. Either we lose a few literal or figurative pounds, congratulate ourselves on our discipline, and then dive headlong back into gorging with a clear conscience; or our initially fervent pledges to control our appetites somehow never quite make the transition from resolution to action.

There are psychological and social explanations for the cultural bulimia that bounces us back and forth between feeding frenzies and compulsive purgings, but we neglect the oscillation's deeper significance if we focus too exclusively upon these two extremes. This is because the root cause of the gorging/purging cycle is the uncomfortable prodding of a trace memory, all but buried under our consumerist obsessions, of two great spiritual truths. The first is that we are indeed creatures who are innately hungry, but hungry for God, not things. The second is that the true nature of the God-hunger that is an essential part of who we are can only be satisfied through fasting, not gorging.

The kind of food we ultimately hunger for is that which genuinely nourishes us and enables us to grow into the sorts of persons we are meant to be. As we saw in the introduction, the nature of a human is such that his or her *telos* is to come to a lived awareness of the divine indwelling spirit. We remain futilely hungry—"restless," as St. Augustine put it—until we recognize that the yearning deep within can only be fulfilled by the God who is our source as well as our end. The problem is that we have forgotten what this innate longing points to— "spiritual fat," as Evagrios Pontikos reminds us, leads to "obtuseness"[6]—and so we scurry to slake our interior craving with substitutes that may temporarily satiate but in the long run fail to sustain. Our hunger inevitably returns, and we just as inevitably resume stuffing ourselves with junk food until we reach a point of uncomfortably bloated saturation, which triggers another dieting binge. The memory trace of the hunger teases us, continuously whetting our appetite, but we've lost sight of what it ultimately points to.

Along with this forgetfulness of the true object of our hunger, we've likewise lost an appreciation of the spiritual truth that the only way to make contact with and hence feed the hunger for God that lies at our core is through fasting. In order to come to a genuine realization of the real nature of

our interior hunger, we must wean ourselves from our distracting craving for junk-food substitutes. It is necessary to
clear the spiritual palate, so to speak, so that its sensitivity is
revitalized. This means, minimally, that we cease frenetically
eating every time we experience hunger pangs, and instead
allow ourselves the opportunity to explore the hunger's true
nature. Occasionally we must starve our worldly appetites in
order to break ground for an excavation of the deeper spiritual hunger beneath them.

Handmaid spirituality's call to fasting invites us to bring
the submerged memories of these two truths to the surface.
Fasting is really a kind of spiritual medicinal. A woman who
desires to bear a child must carefully watch her diet, avoiding
stimulants such as alcohol and tobacco, which she may
crave but which pollute the body and hamper the possibility
of conception. Her refusal to cater to her appetites leads to
withdrawal anxiety, which, in its initial stages, can be quite
unpleasant. But she is willing to endure the self-imposed regimen for the sake of the joy and fulfillment of childbearing.
Similarly, those of us who wish to be Godbearers must refuse
to succumb to cravings that block conception and hamper
fruition. Spiritual fasting is frequently painful, but it is the
price to be paid for the quickening of the divine spirit in our
souls. The pain of fasting opens the door to spiritual renewal:
both sets of contrasting tiles are essential for the rediscovery
of our original image.

Scriptural Insights

Mary's reminder that fasting is a medicinal for spiritual
growth echoes a long scriptural tradition. Both the Old and
the New Testaments teach that fasting is a necessary condition for controlling one's worldly appetites, thus allowing true

God-hunger to blossom. The continuity between the two Testaments on the subject is quite recognizable. But there's also a decided difference in accent or tone between what fasting meant to the Old Testament authors and what it meant to Jesus and the early Church. As we'll see in this section, the New Testament's innovative view of fasting is especially important for Handmaid spirituality.

For the ancient Hebrews, fasting was primarily an act of penance or mourning for unrighteousness in which the entire community participated and was collectively cleansed. The Old Testament makes room for private penitential fasts (e.g., 2 Sm 12:15–23; 1 Kgs 21:27; Ps 69:1–15), but repeatedly we find the norm to be a ceremonial public acknowledgment of spiritual shortfalling. Leviticus (16:31–34) codified the custom by decreeing that an annual Day of Atonement should be observed in which the people of God fast and "afflict" themselves. In addition, national days of fasting were periodically proclaimed (e.g., 2 Chr 20:3, Ezr 8:21–23; Jer 36:9) to recall the Hebrews to God's ways. During these national fasts, people were urged to wear sackcloth as a public symbol of regret for their personal and communal guilt. Days set aside for public fasting were frequently called during times of impending disaster, such as when the prophet Joel (1:14) urged a "solemn assembly" of the "elders and all the inhabitants of the land" in anticipation of the terrible "Day of the Lord." But fast days were also proclaimed to solemnize turning points in the affairs of Israel and Judea: Ezra (8:21) called for a fast to commemorate the rededication of the Temple ("...that we might humble ourselves before our God, to seek from him a straight way for ourselves...."), and Nehemiah (9:1) to commemorate the rebuilding of Jerusalem's walls ("...the people of Israel were assembled with fasting and in sackcloth, and with earth upon their heads...and stood and confessed their sins...").

Fast days, whether prescribed by the religious calendar or proclaimed on special occasions, were intended to redirect an erring people back to the ways of God. They offered opportunities for a spiritual housecleaning in which the penitent was urged to rid him or herself of the burden of accumulated sin so that a conversion experience could occur. The Hebrew word for *conversion,* derived from the root *shub,* literally means a turning back or a retracing of one's steps in order to return to the path of righteousness (more about this in chapter 3). Fasting, then, was a symbolic act of spiritual stock taking aimed at liberating individuals from a false sense of direction in order to reorient them to the ways of God.

For the most part, the ancient Hebrew tradition of fasting demanded doleful and sometimes lugubrious acts of abasement and expiation. But the sixth-century-B.C.E. prophet Zechariah set a new tone. In foretelling the rebuilding of the Temple and the restoration of Zion, he encouraged (8:19) his people to set aside fast days which "shall be to the house of Judah seasons of joy and gladness, and cheerful feasts." Zechariah's purpose was not to downplay the mourning and self-accusation appropriate to spiritual self-examination, but rather to supplement it with an equally proper joy over the reconciliation for which fasting prepared the way.

Zechariah's startling new insight that fasting was an occasion for joyous hope as well as penitential self-denial was revived centuries later by Jesus. Jesus taught his disciples that they need not fast with the austerity or melancholy abjection insisted upon, for example, by the hyperascetic John the Baptist. In the soul cleansing represented by fasting, Jesus said, we prepare ourselves for an invitation to the divine banquet; how could the anticipation of such a delight be the occasion for nothing but sackcloth and ashes?

Additionally, Jesus taught that genuine fasting is a private act of repentance by which the individual truly recognizes and regrets his or her waywardness, and he cautioned that public penitence too frequently substitutes mere ceremonial displays of contrition for authentic heart turnings. The psalmist as well as a few Old Testament prophets, notably Isaiah, had expressed similar reservations, but none had gone so far as to suggest that private fasting should supplant its public counterpart. One of the mainstays of Jesus' ministry, however, was its emphasis on the primacy of interior purification. Thus, he famously warned (Mt 1:1, 17–18) that "practicing...piety before men in order to be seen by them" is a slippery slope to religious hypocrisy, and enjoined his followers to forego showy external displays of lamentation for interior contrition.

The new understanding of fasting taught by Jesus, an understanding that builds upon rather than rejects the Old Testament model, is the authority for Mary's—and Handmaid spirituality's—recognition that authentic Godbearing starts with an inner purging, a frequently painful withdrawal from old eating habits. But it is also shot through with the joyful realization that such denial clears the ground for discovering the true nature of our innate hunger and, consequently, the spiritual food for which we yearn. It is to an examination of this hunger to which fasting seeks to direct us that we must now turn.

Sehnsucht

Even the most gluttonous of us occasionally experience moments in which our hearts ache with such a bittersweet longing that we know the foods we normally gorge on can never satisfy it. We casually decide to take in a movie, but by the time we leave the theater we've been touched in an unexpected way by something in the film that awakens an inarticulate yearning. We happen to overhear a phrase or two from a symphony and swell with vague longings that we can scarcely articulate. A poem we read or hear beckons us to a far country we've never visited but are drawn to with a nostalgia that can only be described as homesickness. We round a curve while driving and suddenly encounter a vista that so overwhelms us with a fleeting glimpse of ultimate fulfillment that we pull over and sit, stunned by what we've just encountered.

These types of experiences share several distinctive characteristics. They are sensory, prompted by an encounter with some aspect of the material realm, but they bowl us over in a way that the merely physical cannot. They strike us as being foreign to our usual way of life, yet somehow also intimately familiar: even as they snatch us from the "everydayness" that is our normal milieu, they have the feel of home about them. Moreover, they overwhelm us with a sense of being close to the center of things, but also reveal to us just how far away we are from it. At one and the same instant they feed and aggravate the hunger deep within. We are replenished but also left unsatisfied by these experiences, and the consequent mixture of fulfillment and incompletion gives rise to an intense craving that bewilders and even frightens us. Matthew Arnold admirably captured the "feel" of such experiences:

> But often, in the world's most crowded streets,
> But often, in the din of strife,
> There arises an unspeakable desire
> After the knowledge of our buried life;
> A thirst to spend our fire and restless force
> In tracking out our true, original course.[7]

When we experience Arnold's moments of "unspeakable desire," we are in the grips of what the German language so aptly refers to as *Sehnsucht:* a longing, a pining, an inarticulate shock of recognition, a nostalgia for one's true home, a soul-hunger. After these moments pass and we return to the normal din of everyday life, we are frequently tempted to write them off as merely emotional reactions—relegating them, for example, to the convenient, catchall category of "aesthetic" experience. But this is a grave mistake, because the flashes of soul-hunger that come unbidden to us are laden with deep meaning and rich promise. It is also futile, because once we have been brushed by their hint of "our true, original course," their memory will haunt us.

What is the meaning and promise toward which moments of *Sehnsucht* so poignantly gesture? Plato gives us a clue in his *Symposium.* In that dialogue he notes that the sensory objects—music, poems, landscapes, and so on—that may trigger *Sehnsucht* cannot in and of themselves satisfy it. This is unnerving because it runs so counter to our normal experiences of longing: the drink and food that attract us when we're parched or hungry, for example, are perfectly sufficient in themselves to satisfy our desire. We feed and are sated. We drink and our thirst is quenched. But *Sehnsucht* is not similarly alleviated. We can feast our eyes for hours on a beautiful landscape, cramming ourselves as full of it as we possibly can, and the desire it stirs in us will not be satisfied. Indeed, paradoxically, the more we feed, the more hungry we feel.[8]

When Plato noted this curious phenomenon twenty-five centuries ago, he concluded that it could only be accounted for by assuming that the concrete object on which *Sehnsucht* rides is not the true object of our longing, but only a dim reflection of it. What attracts us to the poem or the piece of music is the shimmer of something it radiates but does not originate. This additional quality is as ineluctable as it is seductive. When we encounter it, as the twentieth-century mystic Simone Weil said, "We do not in the least know what it is. It is a sphinx, an enigma, a mystery which is painfully tantalizing."[9] Yet it is precisely this mystery—this hint of a "buried life," to use Arnold's expression—present yet just beyond reach, for which we ache. For both Plato and Weil, then, the experience of *Sehnsucht* gestures beyond the object of our immediate attraction to a deeper, ultimately satisfying object of desire that nudges us to search for increasingly intimate encounters with it.

Plato speculated that the enigmatic objects of *Sehnsucht's* yearning are what he called the "Forms"—eternally perfect and utterly impersonal metaphysical principles that serve as the universal archetypes for everything that exists in the everyday temporal realm. When we encounter a beautiful sensory object in the world, for example, we are attracted not by its immediate and transitory beauty, but rather by our vague intuition of the perfect metaphysical Beauty of which it is an imperfect copy. Similarly, we are stirred by individual acts of virtue such as kindness and compassion, because we dimly sense in them an echo of the eternal principle of Goodness which serves as their foundation.

Insightful as Plato's discussion of the mystery of *Sehnsucht* is, it raises a perplexity that subsequent thinkers, including Plato's own student Aristotle, were quick to point out. The problem is that it's not at all clear how the eternal Forms make contact with the temporal world of sensory objects through which humans are able, howsoever dimly, to intuit absolute Goodness or Beauty. Plato's two realms, one of perfect and unchanging Forms, the other of imperfect and transitory objects-in-the-world, seem on the face of things to be so utterly incompatible that it's difficult to see how they could ever intersect. Yet obviously such an intersection must somehow take place if sensory objects indeed reflect the eternal Forms.

This perplexity remains forever unresolved if we stop at Plato's claim that the ultimate object of *Sehnsucht's* desire is an abstract realm of metaphysical archetypes: the chasm between his Forms and the temporal world in which we dwell is simply unbridgeable. But we can salvage his insight that sensory objects awaken in us an insatiable hunger if we substitute the Christian notion of a creative and living God for the Hellenic one of metaphysical Forms. God as Creator and Sustainer of the temporal world is not irremediably separated from his creation as Plato's Forms are separated from the realm of physical objects. On the contrary, the divine signature is present everywhere throughout creation, just as the personality and style of an artist is obvious in his or her painting. God is not identical to the created world, and therein lies his transcendence. But it is his spirit that animates and breathes meaning and structure into the sensory realm, and that spirit continues to pulsate throughout the order of created things. Thus God is also imminent, and all of reality bears the imprint of his incarnational presence. This is why Paul could write to the Romans (1:20) that "ever since the creation of the world [God's] invisible nature...has been clearly perceived in the things that have been made," and the gospelist John (1:14) could celebrate the wondrous fact that God has pitched his tent among us.

When we experience a poignant moment of soul-hunger, then, it is because we sense in back of the worldly object that immediately prompts it the indwelling presence of divine spirit. The wonder is not that we experience *Sehnsucht* at all, but that we don't experience it more often. The poet Gerard Manley Hopkins was quite correct when he wrote in the poem

"God's Grandeur" that "The world is charged with the grandeur of God/It will flame out, like shining from shook foil." Reality is saturated with the *pneuma* that founds and sustains it. When our awareness of it is triggered by sensory objects, it's not because they reflect, as Plato believed, something (the Forms) that is external to them. Rather, that which is the ultimate desire of our hearts breaks forth and reveals itself from *within* them. It is God in our midst.

Paul relates a great mystery when he tells us that all creation groans in travail, awaiting with eager longing its ultimate rebirth in God (Rom 8:22). The psalmist (148) speaks in similar fashion when he conjures the dumb earth and sun and moon and shining stars to praise the Lord. The implication is that inanimate nature is so imbued with the spirit and glory of God that even *it* somehow "senses" his indwelling presence and yearns for an ever deepening union.

How much more, then, must we humans, closest of all God's creation in likeness to him, groan with eager longing to make contact with the divine spirit that percolates through us. When we encounter an object in the world that triggers *Sehnsucht,* the spirit within responds to the spirit without, and the awakened memory of our buried life teases us with a homesick longing. This is our *telos,* just as it is the *telos,* if Paul is correct, of the entire created realm. But the crucial difference between our longing and the groaning of the earth and sun and moon is that we alone are capable of an explicit awareness of it. The earth may "feel" its travail in a chthonic, murky fashion, but our homesickness, although frequently buried under layers of gorging-induced fat, is at least potentially conscious. We are capable, if we but will, of embracing the longing so that it can reveal its deep meaning to us. Put another way, we are able to cooperate with the spirit indwelling both us and the rest of creation, of participating in the actualization of our *telos,* by allowing our bittersweet soul-hunger to lead us where it will. As Gregory of Nyssa reminds us, it knows better than we what we truly crave.

> When the soul at the call of its beloved goes out to look for him whom no name can reach, it learns that it is enamored of one who is inaccessible, and is desirous of one who cannot be grasped. These words strike the soul and wound it with despair, because it believes its search for fullness will never come to an end. But the veil of sadness is taken away from it when it is taught that to go forward continually in its search, and never to cease raising its sights, constitutes the true enjoyment of what it desires.[10]

The Urge-to-Gorge

The problem, as I suggested at the beginning of this chapter, is that we habitually forget the true nature of our hunger. We fail or refuse to let it surface because we're too distracted by our appetite for immediate but transitory gratification. Instead of taking the time to harken to *Sehnsucht,* we glut at the first twinge of desire on whatever's at hand. Satiated for the moment, we predictably delude ourselves into supposing that what we grabbed was what we really wanted, and our obsessive patterns of gorging ingrain ever deeper.

This urge-to-gorge, which blinds us to the true meaning of our hunger, has four distinctive characteristics:

In the first place, gorging is behavior that is both impatient and impetuous. The word, significantly, is derived from the Latin *gorges,* "whirlpool," which conjures up images of a furious motion that indiscriminately sucks everything within reach into its voracious funnel. It's obvious that a whirlpool is relentlessly destructive to its environment. But what's not so immediately apparent is that its activity is also self-destructive: in gobbling up everything in sight, a whirlpool runs the risk of so clogging itself with half-chewed debris that its characteristic spinning stalls from the sheer weight of what it has devoured. But the whirlpool neither knows nor cares about this danger. It will continue feeding until it chokes.

The gorger is similarly furious and indiscriminate in his eating habits. Addicted as he is to immediate satiation, he lacks the patience to reflect on the best way to alleviate his hunger. So he impetuously grabs the first thing that he sees on the menu and has no compunction about demanding seconds and thirds. But in the process he becomes so obsessed with the drive to eat that he frequently continues to stuff himself long after the immediate sting of hunger has disappeared. The inevitable result is that he pulls away from the table spiritually bloated and dyspeptic, too weighed down by his feeding frenzy to realize or even much care that he's harmed himself. St. Peter of Damaskos captures this truth in a startling analogy: "The dog that licks his wound with his tongue is not aware of the pain because of the sweetness, and does not realize that he is drinking his own blood; and the glutton who eats what harms him in both soul and body is not aware of the damage he does himself. All those who are the slaves of passion suffer likewise because of their lack of awareness."[11]

This impatient shortsightedness suggests another characteristic of the urge-to-gorge. The gorger sees no sensible response to the experience of hunger other than feeding. When one is sleepy one goes to bed, when thirsty one drinks, and when hungry one eats. What's the point of depriving yourself when you don't have to? A growling stomach demands to be filled like an itch demands to be scratched. Both, like sexual desire or evacuation, are nonmysterious bodily needs. Ignoring them—or even more bizarrely, from the gorger's perspective, deliberately refusing to satisfy them—is a quite unnecessary disruption of natural urges. From this viewpoint, it might also suggest a perverse or neurotic asceticism.

The gorger sees no larger significance behind his hunger and thus reduces it to a mere bodily or psychological craving because, thirdly, he tends to be literal-minded. Accustomed as he is to feeding his hunger with sensory objects, he presumes that his innate craving is directed exclusively toward them. The truth that his voracious appetite in fact points beyond them to an ultimate object of desire for the most part escapes him. Even when he does experience *Sehnsucht,* he more likely than not seeks to satisfy it by glutting even more furiously on the objects that immediately triggered it. If a particular poem moves him, he devours all the poet's writings. If a landscape has awakened the longing of soul-hunger, he becomes a camping enthusiast. The focus here is on sheer quantity: if *this* poem or *this* landscape doesn't completely satisfy, then perhaps scores of poems or dozens of vistas will. In this way the spiritual gorger tries to fill up on *hors d'oeuvres,* so to speak, because his literalness blocks the recognition that these physical stimuli signal, but are not themselves, the main course.

Finally, and perhaps most perniciously, the gorger suffers from the illusion that he's entirely able to satisfy his hunger on his own steam. This stems at least in part from his literal-mindedness: he "knows" what he craves, and knowledge is power. Since the gorger assumes that his hunger points no farther than its immediate object, all he need do is gain possession of that object. Granted, he may not have the immediate wherewithal to get what he wants, but this isn't the point. The important thing is that he sees himself as confident in his understanding of the true nature of his desires and how to satisfy them.

A Rogues' Gallery

There are many ways in which the urge-to-gorge manifests itself. Some are grossly obvious, others disguised and subtle. We obviously can't examine them all here, but we can gain a better understanding of the spiritual malady of gorging by taking a look at three prototypical gorgers and the junk foods upon which they glut.

Portrait 1: Gordon Gekko and Commodity-Gorging. In the consumerist ocean in which we swim, perhaps the most obvious display of the urge-to-gorge is the obsessive way we strive to accumulate wealth, along with the power and material goodies it brings. Many of us, to one degree or another, scurry to fill our emptiness with bigger houses, faster cars, larger incomes, cellular phones, multiple television sets, increasingly exotic vacations. We suffer, in short, from commodity addiction. We impulsively shop to celebrate when we're happy and to console ourselves when we're depressed. Periodically we suffer from the ill effects of such gluttony: credit cards get maxed out, the toys with which we've surrounded ourselves quickly lose their novelty and hence their appeal, and we are left with a dim sense that our frenetic drive to acquire doesn't really address the true nature of our hunger. When this happens, as I pointed out at the beginning of this chapter, we indulge in equally impulsive bouts of purging—or "dieting"—in order to sort ourselves out. But because we've become so addicted to immediate gratification, our dieting binges are short-lived. Once the immediate financial or conscience crisis passes, we return to our commodity chase.

There is surely no more striking recent portrait of this consumerist urge-to-gorge than *Wall Street,* Oliver Stone's cinematic parable about greed in America. The film scrutinizes the world of high finance, whose distinctive idiom ("arbitrage," "leverage," and so on) is probably arcane to most of us. But there's nothing foreign about the spirit of gluttony that fuels its high-powered wheeling and dealing. We all feel its tug.

Wall Street relentlessly rubs our noses in the consumerist spirit that animates us. The viewer is bombarded with dizzying cinematic sequences of frenzied buying and selling by private and corporate gamblers ravenous for a killing on the market. The characters in this morality play live for the big deal; they only really feel alive when the stock exchange bell rings in another day of whirlwind trading, and they sink back into shadow when the same bell closes the day out. Their lives, their values, their aspirations, their very identities, coalesce around the overwhelming urge to gorge themselves on ever greater quantities of stock, capital, yachts, mistresses, power. Those few who have grabbed the golden ring through a combination of brains, luck, and ruthlessness—the "players," in Wall Street argot—crave even more than they already have. The others, wanna-bes with the same obsessive need-to-possess that fuels the players but without the latter's breaks or brains, are consumed by envy and frustration.

The film's protagonist, Gordon Gekko, is a chilling exemplar of the consumerist gorger. Gekko is a player, a self-made multimillionaire with a richly deserved reputation as a rapacious, cutthroat financial wizard. By anyone's estimation he possesses more money than he'll ever be able to spend. But it's still not enough for Gekko. There will *never* be enough, and Gekko is perfectly willing to corrupt or destroy others in order to gorge at ever more resplendent tables. Moreover, he's utterly unapologetic about both the voraciousness of his appetite and the brutal extremes he'll go to in order to feed it. In what is surely the film's most chilling scene, Gekko chants his credo. "Greed," he unabashedly says, "is good. Greed is right. Greed works. Greed cuts through and captures the essence of the evolutionary spirit. Greed in all its forms—greed for life, for money, for love, knowledge—has marked the upward surge of mankind." The fact that the stockholders to whom Gekko speaks in this scene respond to his words with wild enthusiasm only underscores the unhappy fact that there's some Gekko in all of us. Even those of us who are willing on an abstract (and hence no-risk) level to condemn unscrupulous creatures like Gekko in fact find something incredibly seductive about both his breathtaking success and the chutzpah with which he slashes and burns his way to the top. We are all, to one extent or another, Gekko wanna-bes.

Gordon Gekko, like all of us, is hungry. Yet somewhere along the line he lost the capacity to grasp the true nature of his hunger. His unfulfilled craving drives him to want to consume the entire planet, and like all inveterate gorgers he's convinced that he can. He is absolutely dumbfounded when he runs across anyone not similarly obsessed with conquering the world and writes such pitiful specimens off as "wimps."

But far gone as he is, even Gekko experiences moments of *Sehnsucht* that temporarily stop him in his tracks. The film shows him in one scene, for example, as a doting father, passionately in love with his three-year-old son. We discover in another scene that he has a genuine sensitivity to art, which is neither shared nor valued by his Wall Street cronies. And in one particularly revealing clip, Gekko is struck speechless by the beauty of an ocean sunrise. In each of these a glimpse of the ultimate object of human yearning breaks through the layers of spiritual fat Gekko has accumulated over the years, and for brief seconds he stands transfixed by its promise. But his addictive urge-to-gorge impatiently reasserts itself and pulls him back to the trough. It perverts expressions of his father-love into spending sprees that drown his son in gifts, twists his appreciation of art by driving him to purchase millions of dollars' worth of paintings as investments, and drives him to rupture the potentially transfigurative moment of beauty on the morning beach in order to bark instructions through a cellular phone to one of his henchmen. Gekko, like all gorgers, will not allow himself the initial pain of fasting in order to explore the deeper meaning of his hunger. When moments of *Sehnsucht* break through, they so challenge his illusion of self-control that he quickly derails them.

Portrait 2: Antonio Salieri and Egolatry. Peter Shaffer's remarkable play *Amadeus* provides us with another prototypical manifestation of gluttony—what the philosopher Gabriel Marcel calls *egolatry*—the frenetic need to continuously feed the ego until it replaces God as the individual's center of gravity. This gorging, which stems from what the early Church fathers referred to as *philautia,* or overweening self-love, is elemental; traces of it are discernible in all displays of the urge-to-gorge. As John of Damaskos says, it is the "baleful mother" of "spiritual insensitivity and ignorance."[12] Shaffer's drama is a masterfully distilled exploration of its pernicious effects.

The play's protagonists are two actual eighteenth-century composers: the famous Wolfgang Amadeus Mozart, and his now obscure contemporary Antonio Salieri. A two-hundred-year-old rumor persists to this day that Salieri, unable to live with his consuming envy of Mozart's genius, finally poisoned him. There's almost certainly no truth to this legend, but Shaffer takes the rivalry between the two men as the canvas on which to paint an imaginative portrait of Salieri as an individual consumed with hunger for ego aggrandizement. Although the play is entitled *Amadeus,* it really revolves around Salieri and his manic gorging-on-self.

Salieri, like most of us, is a person caught between the devil and the deep blue sea. On the one hand, he passionately yearns to devote himself to what he palpably senses as the proof of God's presence on earth: music. Even as a child Salieri was captivated by the "absolute beauty" of music— "already when I was ten a spray of sounded notes would make me dizzy almost to falling!"—and vowed to dedicate himself to it, to become the "flute of God." But on the other hand, Salieri's longing to sacrifice himself on the altar of absolute beauty is not entirely selfless. He also wants to reap some worldly perquisites from serving divine beauty—fame, wealth, influence. "Not to deceive you," he tells the audience, "I wanted to blaze like a comet across the firmament of Europe!" But, he quickly adds, "only in one especial way. Music! Absolute music!...music is God's art." We see in this revealing confession a familiar pattern: intense moments of soul-hunger, in this case triggered by the beauty of music, alternating with a ravenous craving for worldly objects of desire. The incompatibility of the two, at least in Salieri's case, paves the way for a spiritual crisis that will eventually destroy him.

In his first years as a composer, Salieri has good reason to think that his vow of dedication to music has been accepted and blessed by God. His rise to fame is meteoric: in short order he is named composer to the Hapsburg court and becomes the darling of both commoners and aristocrats. His music is adored by all; his name is on everyone's lips. Aspiring composers vie for his patronage, beautiful women for his favor. He is the flute of God. It is he—he and he alone—who possesses the talent—no, the sheer *genius!*—to bring into the world absolute musical beauty. His youthful fantasy of becoming a comet in the musical heavens has been surpassed. He is now the veritable sun around which the heavenly bodies revolve.

The extent to which Salieri has closed his heart to the call of *Sehnsucht* for the sake of gorging his ego on the fruits of worldly fame is revealed when he encounters Mozart's music for the first time. The otherworldly beauty of it pierces him, as he tells us, with a shock of recognition that sends him reeling, "gasping for life." In Mozart's music Salieri truly experiences the voice of God, that divine object of ultimate human desire. But coupled with and perverting his yearning is the agony of realizing that it is Mozart, and not himself, who is its creator. Salieri's need to gorge his ego reasserts itself even as he is stunned by the glimpse of the far country vouchsafed him through Mozart's music, and he stumbles home in confused and bitter torment, to plead with God. "Let your voice enter *me!* Let *me* conduct you!...*Let* me!" The accent here is exclusively on Salieri's ravenous hunger to be the mouthpiece of God, not on a celebration of the divine beauty intuited through Mozart's music. His manic egolatry runs roughshod over his *Sehnsucht.*

From this time forward Salieri once and for all substitutes his hunger for fame for the more substantial hunger for God. He declares war on his rival Mozart, vowing to crush him. But Salieri knows it is a war he cannot win, for to destroy Mozart (as he eventually does in Shaffer's drama) and regain his place as the musical solar system's sun, is to deprive himself of the absolute beauty his despised rival creates. Salieri is still sensitive enough to his soul-hunger to know that such beauty is his only chance of redemption, but his ravenous need to stoke the self by gorging on fame inexorably drives him to sacrifice its promise of ultimate fulfillment for the baser one of immediate aggrandizement. So Salieri's self-hunger triumphs; he gorges on the destruction of Mozart, fully aware that his gluttony is perverse but unable to resist the imperative demands of ego.

Portrait 3: The Grand Inquisitor and God-Gorging.
Stone's *Wall Street* reminds us of the materialistic greed all
too common in our consumerist society, and Shaffer's
Amadeus warns against the perils of *philautia*. But there's
yet another way in which the urge-to-gorge reveals itself, one
which is much more subtle—and consequently more insidious—than the heavy-handed pursuit of material objects or
the torments of self-love. It is the pietistic gorging on religion
portrayed in Fyodor Dostoevsky's unnerving parable, "The
Grand Inquisitor."

The story, found in Dostoevsky's masterpiece *The Brothers Karamazov,* is well known. In the sixteenth century, at
the height of the "Holy" Inquisition, Christ returns to earth, to
Seville. He wanders the streets, never speaking a word, but
the people who encounter him there are strangely moved by
the electrifying presence of this silent stranger. In his company they sense a promise of ultimate fulfillment and experience heart stirrings that both exhilarate and disturb them.
But Torquemada, the Grand Inquisitor, an old man who has
devoted his entire life to maintaining the religious status quo,
hears word of the stranger and has him arrested. Upon meet-
ing Jesus, the Grand Inquisitor at once recognizes him and,
startlingly, rebukes him for returning. For over fifteen hundred years, he tells Christ, the "Church" has labored to provide the faithful with the religious fast food they crave.
Humans desire painless and responsibility-free absolution;
organized religion, Torquemada cynically says, has given
them that. They crave spoonfed solutions to their perplexities
and doubts; the "Church" has also granted them this. Above
all, humans demand religious consolations that anesthetize
without challenging or rebuking, and this too, the Grand
Inquisitor tells Jesus, organized religion has given them.

And now, Torquemada spits at Jesus, You return and

threaten to overthrow the careful work of centuries. You awaken in humans a restless yearning for something that far transcends the conventionally pious palliatives they *really* want. You would reactivate in them the bittersweet soul-hunger they've struggled to suppress for over a thousand years, a longing the Church has tamed with the easily digestible substitute foods of dogmatic theology and soporific ceremony. I cannot allow You to destroy the peace of mind so laboriously achieved, concludes the Inquisitor, and he promises Jesus that "tomorrow I shall condemn Thee and burn Thee at the stake as the worst of heretics. And the very people who have today kissed Thy feet, tomorrow at the faintest sign from me will rush to heap up the embers of Thy fire."

Dostoevsky's haunting tale is so rich that any number of lessons can be mined from it. But at its deepest level it is a story that reminds us how tempting it is to gorge on religious platitudes and thereby miss God. The consumerist and egolatrous gorging that breeds Gordon Gekkos and Antonio Salieris has its religious parallel, and this is the point Dostoevsky wants to drive home. Just as we allow commodities or ego to derail our soul-hunger, so we can also feed so obsessively on conventional religious symbols and practices that we insulate ourselves against a soul-shaking encounter with the living spirit toward which they point.

We would do well to avoid the mistake of supposing that Dostoevsky's point is to condemn *in toto* religious symbols, creeds, or institutionalized modes of worship. Nor is he indulging in typical nineteenth-century (or twentieth-century, for that matter!) church bashing; he was, after all, a fervently loyal son of Russian Orthodoxy.[13] Dostoevsky is quite convinced that conventional expressions of religious faith can and do nurture a genuine growth in God. But he is painfully aware that they can also be corrupted by a spirit of religious consumerism into a shallow piety that substitutes the quick fix of religious fetishism for authentic interiority. This comfortable religiosity might make for good "church people," but it hardly breeds good Christians.

The point is that many persons who consider themselves religious are no more eager than anyone else to forego immediate gratification. So instead of realizing that conventional churchly idioms are the specifically religious triggers of *Sehnsucht,* they take the easy way out by regarding them as ends in themselves. The spiritual gorger gluts himself on the letter rather than the spirit, sating his hunger with ever more unctuous observances of holy days, rotely mechanical recitations of formulaic prayers, and unreflective nods to doctrinal credos. Feeding on these foods rather than the ultimate object of desire to which they are intended to lead us gives the gorger the pleasant illusion of fulfilling religious obligations without having to endure the painful challenge of going beyond them to stand before the ultimate mystery. But such consolations, as Dietrich Bonhoeffer cautioned, are "cheap grace," self-serving albeit piously phrased demands for God's blessings, which require nothing from us in return.[14] They may do something in the short run to palliate our soul-hunger, but their long-term soporific effects atrophy our relationship with God by transforming his living presence, as the poet Wallace Stevens chillingly wrote, into

> A face of stone...,
> An effulgence faded...,
> Too venerably used. That might have been.
> It might and might have been.

Elsewhere Stevens warns that the fast food of cheap grace makes a parakeet of the Paraclete and transforms the roaring lion of Judah into a "cat of...sleek transparency."[15] Archbishop of Canterbury William Temple sounded a similar note when he once scandalized his flock by cautioning them that it is a grave mistake to suppose that God is exclusively or even primarily interested in "religion." But the insights of Bonhoeffer, Stevens, and Temple escape the spiritual gorger. He prefers a self-righteous munching on stale religious platitudes to the healthier food of manna.

Still, regardless of how sanctimoniously bloated a spiritual gorger becomes, there are moments of opportunity when the *Sehnsucht* that incessantly prods him toward God breaks through, and the blueprinted ritualisms and comfortable pieties on which he normally feeds no longer completely satisfy. Even the Grand Inquisitor, who so desperately wishes to spare his flock and himself the bittersweet restlessness of soul-hunger, occasionally knows deep within his heart that he's taken the wrong path. One of these moments of yearning hits Torquemada at the close of his denunciatory interrogation of Jesus. After bitterly haranguing his silent prisoner for returning to earth and disrupting the easy spirituality he has labored so long to codify, the Grand Inquisitor, so Dostoevsky tells us, "longed for Him to say something, however bitter and terrible. But He suddenly approached the old man in silence and softly kissed him on the forehead." At that moment the Grand Inquisitor is flooded with a piercing awareness of just how much he has given up by his lifelong feeding on symbol rather than substance. The old man shuddered with the ache of it, and carried in his heart the memory of Christ's kiss for the rest of his days. He would continue to feed on canon law, on formulaic worship, on easily digestible religiosity; the habit was too ingrained, and the Grand Inquisitor too fearful of going beyond these conventions to embrace his soul-hunger. But he never forgot the glimpse of a far and wonderful country vouchsafed him in Christ's embrace.

Thinking "Big"

C. S. Lewis once observed that the problem with many of us is that our appetites aren't large enough. "We are half-hearted creatures," he wrote, "fooling about with drink and sex and ambition when infinite joy is offered us, like an ignorant child who wants to go on making mud pies in a slum because he cannot imagine what is meant by the offer of a holiday at sea. We are far too easily pleased."[16]

This is a brilliant spiritual insight—and it echoes, by the way, St. Teresa of Avila's equally illuminating one that the more we ask of God the greater we honor Him—because it helps to explain what holds gorgers such as Gekko or Salieri or Torquemada back from moving beyond immediate objects of desire. They—we—do not allow the hunger within to reach the point where it can be slackened only by God. Our innate appetites are cosmic. But our habit of settling for less than that which fully satisfies shrinks our spiritual bellies, so to speak, until they are incapable of holding more solid fare. In glutting ourselves on junk food we weary our palate and jade our desires until we aim no higher than that which is immediately at hand. We do harm to ourselves, as Mary reminds us in her Medjugorje message. We are like the Samaritan woman at the well in John's Gospel (4:7–15) who is so accustomed to worldly water that her more profound thirst for the living water of the spirit is all but forgotten.

Doubtlessly, part of the reason why we balk at allowing our *Sehnsucht* to take us where it will is anxiety about traveling beyond the familiar contours of everydayness. As we saw with Torquemada's refusal to explore the deeper meaning of institutionalized religious trappings (or, in the introduction, Mary's initially fearful reaction to Gabriel's proclamation of her as *Theotokos*), the prospect of forsaking customary objects of desire to pursue the ultimate one is wrenching. But the primary reason for our failure to heed soul-hunger is, quite simply, the spiritual inertia born from stunted appetites. The nineteenth-century philosopher Søren Kierkegaard observed that the person who frenziedly feeds at the trough of sensual and worldly pleasures will soon blunt his capacity for either desire or enjoyment. Like the world-weary and jaded Don Juan, he may continue to go through the motions of gorging out of sheer habit, but he has little appetite for his food and derives even less satisfaction from it. His sensitivity has been debauched.[17]

When a gorger has reached this point, one of three things is likely to happen. He can sink into a dazed and weary indifference—the traditional fate of the libertine who in his youth so glutted on the world's pleasures that he ends his days in bloated semiconsciousness. But if this occurs, to go back to an image of Origen's mentioned in the introduction, he allows the spring of living waters within him to silt over. Or he can try to jump-start his failing appetite and desires by frantically cramming in larger and spicier quantities of junk food. This, of course, is the route that Gordon Gekko, Antonio Salieri, and Torquemada follow: Gekko's jaded appetite desperately insists on more and more money, Salieri's on a progressively inflated ego, and Torquemada's on an increasingly rigid fidelity to cheap grace. But walking this path will break the heart, because such objects of desire can never ultimately satisfy the craving within. They are only, as Lewis says, "the scent of a flower we have not found, the echo of a tune we have not heard, news from a country we have never yet visited."[18] Or, finally, the gorger can relinquish his proud confidence that he knows best how to satisfy his hunger, accept a purgative regimen of fasting, and allow his reawakened *Sehnsucht* to lead him to the buried God within. This, of course, is the choice of those who follow the Handmaid's way.

Stated differently, the gorger can wean himself from his incessant need to glut by "thinking big." Heeding the advice of Lewis and Teresa, harkening to the story of the woman at the well, and reverentially following the Blessed Virgin's example, he can renounce his acquired small and petty appetites for the sake of the colossal one with which he was born. "Thinking big" here should not be understood in *quantitative* terms; it doesn't mean setting one's sights on more and more commodities or self-aggrandizement, much less a quasi-magical warehousing of daily prayers and holy relics. Instead, "thinking big" in the spiritual sense means cultivating an appetite for that which is *qualitatively* ultimate, the object of desire promising absolute fulfillment, extending to us the assurance that whoever drinks its waters will never thirst again. And that, of course, can only be God. If we indeed honor God by asking for big favors, the highest honor we give him is asking for himself.

Embracing the Hunger

As we've seen, the urge-to-gorge prevents us from exploring and growing from the soul-hunger deep within, and this in turn renders us barren and unable to join with Mary in the great task of Godbearing to which we are called. Fasting is that *ascesis,* or spiritual exercise, by which we combat the gluttony that vitiates us. It offers us a regimen by which to shed surplus weight—the fat of spiritual obtuseness—so that we may grow into our roles as *Theotokoi.* "Let us cherish fasting," then, as St. Athanasius says, "for fasting is the great safeguard....Just as Adam was driven out of paradise for having eaten, refusing to trust, so it is by fasting...that they who wish to enter paradise do so."[19]

Sacred scripture teaches us how to fast. As noted earlier in this chapter, both testaments view fasting as a process of penitential relinquishment in which the individual detaches herself from those appetites that turn her face from God. It encourages a spiritual stock-taking which allows us to remember and live Plato's fundamental insight that immediate objects of desire are only dim reflections of that for which we truly yearn. In so doing, fasting liberates us from the pernicious cycle of gorging and dieting and opens us to God's healing grace.

The *ascesis* of fasting fuels and in turn is fueled by three interrelated responses to the proddings of our innate soul-hunger. They are contrition, resolute renunciation, and trust.

Contrition. The conventional meaning of *contrition* is the experience of sorrow or grief for wrongdoing. But it's instructive to keep in mind that the word is derived from the Latin verb *conterere,* "to bruise." It is an obstinate fact of human nature that we typically refuse to take a close look at our lives until extraordinary circumstances so bruise our normal complacency and smugness that we are forced to reevaluate our priorities. Pain is a remarkably effective incentive to self-examination and spiritual stock-taking.

God employs many tactics to bruise our vain illusions of self-sufficiency and draw us to him, but two of the most obvious are despair and longing. Both are great iconoclasts; they expose the artificiality of our idols of pride and self-reliance and reveal to us just how vulnerable and broken we actually are. They are moments of divine invitation, of sacred opportunity, for the emergence of contrition. Both shatter the everydayness on which we avidly feed by showing that there is a depth to existence we have hitherto ignored. In moments of despair the depth manifests itself as abyss, and when we find ourselves falling into its blackness we come face to face with the poverty of our hitherto cherished appetites. We recognize the material wealth and power, adulation of self, and shallow trappings of conventional piety we once thought would sustain us for what they in fact are: mere ephemera, wisps, illusion. We realize how self-deceived we've been, the extent to which we've corrupted ourselves through the arrogantly indulgent pursuit of objects of desire that offer no real sustenance in times of trial. From the bruising depths of our despair we acknowledge and bitterly regret just how far we've strayed from our true foundation, our true nourishment.

But sometimes depth reveals itself not as abyss but as ground. This occurs, as we've seen, in moments of *Sehnsucht.* God's grandeur flames out like shook foil from behind the veil of sensory objects and sets our hearts ablaze with longing. In those moments, fleeting as they are, we feel with an intensity that shakes us to our core just how distant the usual objects of our desire are from the glimpse of ultimate fulfillment we've been vouchsafed. That vision of a far country bruises us, not only on account of the bittersweet yearning it births, but also because we understand that our own spiritually anemic appetites have closed its borders to us. This horrible realization is often too much to bear, and we quickly block it from our minds by throwing ourselves back into gorging. But sometimes, as happened when Jesus embraced the Grand Inquisitor, the experience so burns in our hearts that, along with St. Peter of Damaskos, we cry out in genuine repugnance and sorrow at our self-imposed exile: "Alas, what shall I do? Where shall I flee from myself? For I am the cause of my own destruction."[20]

Contrition, whether precipitated by despair or longing, is the entrance fee required from us in order to begin the regimen of fasting. It is the moment in which the bruised heart finally breaks, confesses its vulnerability, and acknowledges its waywardness. The soul stands naked, stripped of its brittle armor and shivering with remorse. And in this moment of self-insight, genuine hope is born, for the soul knows within its depths that God, as the psalmist reminds us, will not despise a broken and contrite heart.

Resolute Renunciation. Contrition is a necessary condition for authentic fasting, but it is not sufficient. The awareness of waywardness impressed upon the bruised soul, if it is not to devolve into mere self-hatred or be sloughed off as a passing bad moment, must give rise to a genuine desire to live in such a way as to repair one's brokenness. This is done by weaning ourselves from the worldly objects of desire that have so spiritually jaded us and robbed us of our appetite for the ultimate object of desire.

Make no mistake about it: renunciation is a painful task because it entails the breaking of ingrained gorging habits. Anyone who has ever tried to kick the tobacco addiction, for example, appreciates how difficult it is to liberate oneself not just from the mechanical act of lighting up a cigarette but also, after the immediate withdrawal pains have passed, from the lingering desire for nicotine. It's not uncommon for ex-smokers to experience twinges of tobacco hunger. Long after they think they're conquered the habit they're sometimes disconcerted upon awakening in the morning to recall that their dreams were filled with pleasant visions of smoking. Habits die hard, and the desires that fuel habits are even more obstinate.

But for all that, habits *can* be broken if the addict has reached the point in his or her life where repugnance outweighs craving. The broken and contrite heart yearns for liberation from its self-induced enslavement and accepts as bitter necessity the pain of doing battle. But the struggle must be undertaken with patience and resolve, one step at a time.

The contrite gorger who longs to free herself from her worldly hunger in order to embrace ultimate hunger must first strive to literally detach herself from the spiritual junk foods that tempt her. If her appetite is for wealth and fame, she must remove herself from those situations that predictably exacerbate her craving. She must force herself to pull back from the latest moneymaking scheme that promises worldly payoff but spiritual impoverishment. If the urge-to-gorge manifests itself as *philautia* (and recall that all gorging to a greater or lesser extent does), the contrite gorger must throw herself into situations that focus her attention and energies on others instead of self. If her appetite is for the cheap grace of shallow religiosity, the gorger must steel herself to forego the conventional "spiritual" exercises that palliate her hunger. The ultimate goal, of course, is not a detachment from things of the spirit, but rather from the feel-good substitutes that provide easy consolation.

These rather mechanical separations of the gorger from the objects of her addictive desires obviously are not adequate in themselves to liberate her from the ingrained habits of years, and it is a grave mistake to suppose otherwise. Merely distancing oneself in an external manner from objects of desire is a first step, but it does not constitute genuine fasting unless it eventually culminates in an internal relinquishment of the craving for them. The urge-to-gorge is not overcome if we are still enslaved by desire for the junk foods we no longer eat. As St. Peter of Damaskos reminds us, "Love of possessions consists not merely in owning many things, but also in *attachment* to them."[21] We must renounce not only the *objects* of desire, but also the very *desire* itself.

In order to reach the point where we are liberated from the craving as well as the actual indulgence in addictive objects of desire, our renunciation must be resolute. Persistence is the key to breaking bad habits; without it our efforts to fast quickly corrupt into sporadic purging and the cycle of gorging/dieting is reestablished. We can externally distance ourselves from objects of desire through a sheer act of will—aided, of course, by grace. But the habit of interior craving can finally be broken only if it is replaced by an habituation to abstinence.

Aristotle recognized this when he argued that the way to become a virtuous person was by habituating oneself to virtue. Force yourself, he advised, to go through the motions of virtuous behavior, even if your heart isn't in it, even if your inner desires nudge you in the opposite direction. Sooner or later you will grow so accustomed to behaving virtuously that what once was a burdensome act of the will becomes second nature. When this happens, the desire to act nonvirtuously begins to dissipate. Further habituation to good acts, Aristotle predicted, will eventually lead to a realization on the part of the practitioner that virtue is more conducive to fulfillment and happiness than vice. When this happens, one's desires will inevitably shift to virtue.[22]

The spiritual process of fasting operates similarly. The more we refuse to indulge in junk food, the more accustomed we grow to doing without it. The steady liberation from the spiritual obtuseness it breeds leads us ever nearer to an appreciation of the true object of our hunger, and our interior growing desire for that object inevitably replaces our gluttonous craving for sensory pleasures. What originally was a painful renunciation blossoms forth as a celebratory embrace. Diadochus of Photike insightfully reminds us that "we do not readily despise the delights of this life if we do not taste with complete satisfaction the sweetness of God."[23] But once we have supped at the divine banquet, even if we are seated "below the salt," at the very foot of the table, we are never willing to resume our old eating habits.

Trust. Fasting, as the Old Testament acknowledges, is a difficult business. The gorging habit dies hard; the flesh asserts itself again and again. Thus the importance of persistence.

But because we tend to be goal-oriented creatures, persistence comes hard unless there is assurance that our sacrifices, to put it crudely, have some payoff. It's true that our failure to heed the call of *Sehnsucht* arises in part from self-indulgence and the inertia born from habit. But it can scarcely be denied that we also write off such moments as mere passing moods because we are wary about investing too much of ourselves in them. They frequently strike us as too subjective, too intensely private, too ephemeral, to take seriously. We demand warranty that the experiences truly point to something beyond wishful thinking before we commit to them. In short, we demand proof of their trustworthiness.

But the unreasonableness of this position becomes apparent if we think for a moment about what it means to trust. When we trust in another person, for example, we typically don't separate ourselves from interactions with that person and scrutinize her behavior in a detached, impersonal way, withholding ourselves until she has "proven" herself worthy of our confidence. On the contrary, we make ourselves available to her because we sense something about her that suggests the gamble is worth the risk. As we expose more of ourselves to her in the development of the relationship, and she in turn reveals more of herself to us, we test whether or not our initial gamble was a good one by reflecting on the ways in which the relationship has affected us. Sometimes the change is good, sometimes not. But the only way we can finally come to a conclusion one way or another is through risky engagement, not defensive standoffishness. In other words, trust arises, when it does, from throwing ourselves into the lived experiment of trusting. The detached spectator who invests nothing of himself will never be able to gather enough abstract evidence to "prove" another person's trustworthiness.

And such is the case with trust in that far country to which *Sehnsucht* calls us. If we insist on absolute proof of its reality as a condition of our beginning the journey, we shall never be able to take moments of soul-hunger seriously enough to leave our homesteads. But if we risk making ourselves available to the soul-hunger, engaging heart, mind, and soul in order to explore more fully the promise vaguely sensed in it, the ensuing spiritual growth guarantees that the risk is worth taking. The BBC production of William Nicholson's *Shadowlands,* a drama about C. S. Lewis and Joy Davidman, expresses this insight well. At one point in the play, Nicholson has Lewis ask Joy if she's ever dived. Joy can't make out what Lewis is driving at. "Dived?" she asks in bewilderment. Yes, Lewis responds, dived. Before one actually steels up courage to take the plunge, he says, the prospect of diving seems foolishly dangerous. How can one be assured that he won't drown in a swift current or be dashed on hidden rocks? The natural inclination is to pull back and examine nautical maps that plumb the water's depths. But even if one were to do that, the wariness would remain. No, the only way to trust that one will not come to grief is simply to dive. Once one actually does it, it's the easiest thing in the world.[24]

Fasting is an experiment in trust. The *Sehnsucht* that beckons to us must be embraced—dived into headfirst—rather than abstractly (and safely) scrutinized from the outside. But this doesn't mean that we are completely without guidance, because the experience of soul-hunger, like the encounter with a person to whom we find ourselves attracted, carries with it the reassuring aroma of promise. This, in fact, is what initially attracts us to it, and "trust" is precisely the testing of the promise.

In the first place, the experience of *Sehnsucht* holds out the assurance that our efforts to shed the layers of spiritual fat accumulated by the urge-to-gorge are collaborative rather than solitary. In the lifelong process of Godbearing to which Handmaid spirituality calls us, the initiative is always God's. Our task is to realize our true natures by allowing the Godseed within to quicken, but the seed itself—and, ultimately, our ability to participate in its gestation—comes from God. Daunting as the prospect of fasting in order to embrace soul-hunger might be, we have the assurance that we do not engage in the *ascesis* by ourselves. The divine spirit is always present, nudging us, guiding us, uplifting us. We are not alone.

Second, as Jesus' words in the New Testament remind us, fasting is really a cause for joyful celebration, in spite of the withdrawal pains it brings. The liberation from our addictive gluttony offered by fasting is a preparation for richer encounters with the soul-hunger deep within—and, consequently, for the ultimate encounter with God, the final object of our hunger, the *telos,* which is ours by virtue of who we are. This is God's promise to us, guaranteed by the experiences of the saints and, of course, by the Blessed Mother.

It's a misunderstanding of fasting, then, to suppose that it is nothing more than a relentless nay-saying, a gloomy and tight-jawed repudiation of the things of the world. There *is* that side to it, true: fasting calls upon us to renounce our ingrained habits of gorging, and until we conquer them we must steel ourselves to a certain amount of painful denial. But this is not a renunciation of the world—which after all is aglow with the shimmer of God—so much as a relinquishment of our obsessive appetite that sells the world short. Denial is never an end in itself; instead, it is a method we trust to make our appetites worthy of the divine banquet we are promised. St. Athanasius is quite correct when he cautions that an "extreme ascesis which risks making your body feeble and useless" is not genuine fasting but a refusal to trust in divine grace[25]—to "dive," as Lewis put it. Diadochus of Photike declares that the goal of fasting is a celebratory embrace of life, and one can scarcely achieve this if body and soul are compulsively punished. Invoking Paul's comparison of spiritual growth to a race, Diadochus reminds us that "the athlete must not be in poor shape."[26]

Fasting, then, is a grand yea-saying, a celebratory, trustful embrace of what is truly important, of that which brings genuine joy rather than temporary satiation. As we grow into the way of fasting and discover how it transfigures our lives and the world around us, we gain abundant reason to trust that the immediate pain is a preparation for greater rejoicing.

Recollection

One of the great treasures of Western literature is Homer's story of Odysseus's long and arduous journey on the wine-dark sea of self-discovery. Separated from the object of their hearts' yearning, Odysseus and his men wandered through many strange lands and endured many perilous adventures in search of it. They encountered great dangers in their wayfaring, which tested their courage and endurance to the breaking point. But the deadliest of all their adversaries was not the bewitchments of a Circe or the primordial fury of a Cyclops. It was a flower, lovely to behold and sweet to the tongue.

After years of apparently fruitless wandering, and immediately after managing to pull out of a nine-day battle with teeming sea and dangerous winds, Odysseus and his exhausted and heartsick crew chance upon the coastline of a beautiful island. Odysseus sends three men out to explore and report back, but they fail to return. When he goes after them, he discovers to his horror that his ship has washed ashore on the legendary Isle of the Lotos Eaters. The Lotos Eaters are a race of people who sup exclusively on the "honeyed plant" of the lotos, which has the peculiar property of inducing forgetfulness in all who partake of it. The sweetness of the lotos is almost overwhelmingly seductive, and its narcotic effect of satiated tranquility so pleasing that travel-stained wanderers who eat of the plant never resume their journeys.

The three men Odysseus sent to explore the island have eaten of the lotos and succumbed to its enslavement. Homer tells us that "they longed to stay forever, browsing on that native bloom, forgetful of their homeland." But Odysseus drives them, all three wailing, back onto the waiting ship and ties them to its rowing benches. Then he urgently summons the rest of his crew. "All hands aboard!" he shouts. "Come, clear the beach and no one taste the Lotos, or you lose your hope of home!" Centuries after Homer chanted the tale, the Victorian poet Tennyson tried to capture in verse the terrible allure the lotos plant had for Odysseus's travel-weary crew:

> They sat them down upon the yellow sand,
> Between the sun and moon upon the shore;
> And sweet it was to dream of Fatherland,
> Of child, and wife, and slave; but evermore
> Most weary seem'd the sea, weary the oar,
> Weary the wandering fields of barren foam.
> Then some one said, 'We will return no more';
> And all at once they sang, 'Our island home
> Is far beyond the wave; we will no longer roam.'[27]

There is a great truth that shines forth in this haunting parable of the lotos eaters. Like Odysseus and his crew, all of us pine with nostalgia for the home from which we've strayed in this journey called life. Weary and heartsick with travel, sometimes fearing we shall never find our way, occasionally suspecting that our dim memories of home are mere fancies, we seek haven in the land of the lotos eaters. We partake of that isle's seductive fruit, first timidly and then rapaciously, and sink gratefully into its soft bed of forgetfulness. We forsake the restless soul-hunger within for the immediate satiation which the magical plant offers us. Occasionally, memories of child and spouse flood back into our consciousness, burning there with an ache so painful that we're jolted out of our lotos-induced reverie. So we stuff ourselves anew until the yearning evaporates and we once again forget. But we build up resistance to the lotos, as we do to all narcotics, and find ourselves needing to glut more frequently on greater quantities of it in order to sustain our placid amnesia. In quick order we find ourselves enslaved by the very food we once trusted to save us.

We are lotos eaters, you and I, forgetful either through perversity or weakness of who we are and where we belong, greedily willing to trade our birthright for a mess of pottage. We carry within our hearts a recollection of our one true home, but all too often gorge ourselves into a bloated forgetfulness of it. The spiritual discipline of fasting urged upon us by Mary's Medjugorje messages seeks to recall us to mindfulness of that for which we truly hunger, for our "island home...far beyond the wave." Handmaid spirituality teaches us how to escape the lure of the urge-to-gorge by embracing rather than fleeing from the hunger for God which essentially defines us. Neither the pain nor the joyful promise of fasting constitute ends in themselves, but they *are* the first grace-filled movements of the Godseed within. If we endure their labor pains with mindfulness and expectation, we can grow into the *Theotokoi* we are meant to be. This is not the path of the gorger, of the lotos eater. But it is the Handmaid's way.

Chapter Two

Prayer

My soul magnifies the Lord....
                              Luke 1:46

God is offering himself to you
in fullness and you can discover
him only in prayer.
                              Medjugorje
                              25 February 1990

Pray without ceasing.
                              1 Thessalonians 5:17

"Flowers for Heaven"

Handmaid spirituality seeks to teach us how to collaborate in the quickening of Godseed. As we saw in the previous chapter, fasting is the first step in this direction because it weans us from our cloying addictions to worldly desires and helps us recollect the true meaning of our innate hunger. It nudges us to embrace the hunger, both its promise and its pain, rather than to flee it as is our wont. When we do so we discover a depth to existence that inevitably awakens in us a longing for richer communion with it. Prayer is the way by which we open our hearts to that depth.

Prayer has always been at the heart of the Christian life. It retains its centrality in Handmaid spirituality; the Blessed Mother speaks of prayer at Medjugorje more frequently than either fasting or conversion. A common refrain in her messages to the world is the plea to "pray, pray, pray!"[1] "Pray, dear children, without ceasing,"[2] she urges, and gently chastises us for being "asleep in prayer."[3] Too frequently we either ignore prayer or simply go through the motions of mouthing formulaic words that mean little or nothing to us. But Mary invites us to be "more attentive,"[4] "to pray with the heart and not only by habit,"[5] to be "active" instead of mechanical in prayer,[6] and to place prayer at the center of our existence rather than relegating it to the periphery. "Let prayer be life to you...grow from day to day through prayer, always toward God."[7]

Prayer is central to Handmaid spirituality's goal of God-bearing because, as Mary tells us through the Medjurgorje visionaries, we "cannot open [our]selves to God" without it.[8] "Without prayer you cannot feel me, nor God, nor the graces I am giving you."[9] Prayer encourages the growth of a spiritual sensitivity to the wellspring of living water within, thus enabling us to "encounter" the divine spirit that indwells us and all creation.[10] It is the necessary next step in our transformation into *Theotokoi*,[11] a transfiguration for which the heightened receptivity nurtured by fasting has prepared the way. As Evagrios Pontikos noted in the early years of Christianity, "The prayer of one who fasts is an eagle in full flight. That of the [glutton] is made heavy with satiety and dragged down to earth."[12]

In communicating the benefits of prayer, Mary doesn't appeal to the image of a soaring eagle herself. But the metaphor she does invoke is just as expressive and more in keeping with the maternally nurturing temperament of Handmaid spirituality.

When you pray, dear children, you become more beautiful. You become like flowers, which after the snow show
forth their beauty, and whose colors become indescrib-
able. And so you, dear children, after prayer before God
display everything that is beautiful so that you may
become beloved by Him....[P]ray and open yourself to
God so that He may make of you a harmonious and
beautiful flower for heaven.[13]

These words harken back to Handmaid spirituality's signature insight that all of us hold Godseed within our hearts, and
that the ultimate purpose of human existence is to collaborate in its fruition. The seed typically lies buried in the sterile
snowbanks of our self-will and forgetfulness. But once fasting
has tilled the soil of our hearts, prayer ushers in a springtime
whose warmth invites the Godseed to quicken and gestate,
preparing us for a blossoming into the "harmonious and
beautiful" flowers we are meant to be. The seed is the vine, as
Jesus reminded us, and we its branches. When the vine flour-
ishes, we cannot but do likewise.

This chapter explores the nature and practice of prayer,
and its essential role in Godbearing. As we'll discover, the
essence of prayer is a reverential listening to the holy silence
that envelopes God. Perhaps the greatest obstacle to genuine
prayer is our insistence on talking too much. But prayer is not
primarily worded. It is lived. Mary's way teaches us that our
spiritual destiny, the blossoming-forth of harmonious and
beautiful soul-flowers, is not a *speaking* of prayer. It is
becoming prayer.

Conversing with God

As in the case of fasting, the ultimate authority for Handmaid spirituality's understanding of prayer is sacred scripture.

Both the Old and the New Testaments concur that prayer is essentially a listening to the divine spirit. Prayer may, of course, perform a number of different functions: petitioning, praising, thanking, confessing. But each of these implies a conversation between God and the person who prays—Mary herself tells us at Medjugorje that prayer is "a conversation with God"[14]—and a genuine conversation only emerges from careful, attentive listening.

This notion of prayer as listening is introduced quite early in the Bible. God converses with Adam (Gn 3:9-12), Abraham (Gn 15:1-6), and Moses (Ex 3:1-4), as well as with kings (1 Sm 23:2-4) and prophets (Jer 1:4-19). It's worth pointing out that in nearly all these examples it is God who initiates the dialogue; the exception (in 1 Sm) is David's plea for counsel about how to make war against the Philistines. But it's equally important to note that each of the persons engaged in these prayerful conversations with God had been prodded by his particular circumstances to listen with sensitivity. Adam's sense of guilt, Abraham's worry about the future of his line, Moses' awe-struck wonderment at the burning bush, Jeremiah's disgust over injustice and unrighteousness, David's fear for his very life: each of these crises heightened receptivity to the divine voice.

Two valuable lessons about the nature of prayer can be gleaned from these Old Testament stories. The first is that God is neither aloof nor dumb, but speaks in and to his creation. The second is that human sensitivity to God's voice is increased when we're shaken out of our normal complacency by either a spiritual crisis or an intense flash of *Sehnsucht*. Such experiences reveal to us our radical dependency, and this in turn opens the ears of the heart.

The problem, of course, is that we're usually too preoccupied to heed another's voice, be it God's or a fellow human's.

We are eager talkers but poor listeners, and scripture is replete with reminders of this unhappy fact. Jeremiah (5:21) chastises a "foolish and senseless people...who have ears, but hear not." The author of Proverbs (2:2) less harshly counsels us to make our ears attentive to wisdom—that is, the Holy Spirit—and to incline our hearts to understanding. (St. Benedict picks up on this in the evocative first line of his *Rule:* "*Obsculta, O fili, praecepta magistri, et inclina aurem cordis tui*"—"Listen carefully, children, to the master's instructions, and attend to them with the ear of your heart.") And Jesus admonishes his followers again and again (e.g., Mt 11:15, 13:9; Lk 14:35; Rv 2:29) to open their ears and attend carefully to his words: Let those with ears listen!

The unhappy consequences of not listening are graphically portrayed time and again in scripture. Just as gorging leads to spiritual obtuseness, so a refusal to listen leads to spiritual deafness. This is surely one of the points in Mark's (6:1–6) retelling of Jesus' rejection by the people of his own village. Mark relates that one Sabbath day Jesus began teaching in his hometown's synagogue and "many who heard him were astounded." Their astonishment wasn't born of awe at the wisdom and insight of his words, however, but rather of the arrogance that accompanies spiritual deafness. "Where did this man get all this?" they scornfully cried. "What is this wisdom that has been given to him?...Is not this the carpenter, the son of Mary and brother of James and Joses and Judas and Simon, and are not his sisters here with us?" The Nazarenes' obstinate refusal to open themselves up to Jesus' words resulted in a squandered opportunity for harkening to the divine voice. They drowned out the voice with the din of their limited sense of propriety and their unbending preconceptions—a hazard, as we shall see shortly, still very much present today. The consequence was that they barricaded their hearts against the quickening of God-seed. As Mark tells us, Jesus could perform no deed of power there. God's transformative Word can only be heard if we are willing to listen.

But what happens when we open the ears of our hearts in prayer? A clue is found in another of Mark's stories, this time in Christ's healing of the deaf man. According to Mark (7:32–35),

> [the disciples] brought to [Jesus] a man who was deaf and had an impediment in his speech; and they besought him to lay his hand upon him. And taking him aside from the multitude, privately, he put his fingers into his ears, and he spat and touched his tongue; and looking up to heaven, he sighed, and said to him, "Eph-phatha," that is, "Be opened." And his ears were opened, his tongue was released, and he spoke plainly.

Several insights about what it means to listen/pray emerge from this story. To begin with, it reminds us that the act of listening to the divine call is essentially a private engagement between the individual and God: Jesus takes the deaf man away "from the multitude, privately." This recalls other New Testament passages in which Christ advises us to go into a shuttered room and pray in secret (Mt 6:6), or when he sets an example for us by retreating into the hills to pray by himself (e.g. Mt 14:23). This doesn't mean that we cannot pray in communion with other worshipers, or that liturgical expressions of prayer are somehow less legitimate than private ones. After all, the deaf man first encountered Jesus through the mediation of others who introduced him to the Messiah. But it does remind us that even when we kneel with others in formal liturgical settings to listen to God, the listening is an intensely private affair between ourselves and the divine. It is ultimately through our own ears that we must listen.

Moreover, the story in Mark's Gospel reminds us that the act of listening is always in response to an initiative from God. God lays his hands upon our hearts just as Jesus laid his upon the deaf man's ears, and awakens within them a sensitivity to his presence. True, we can and should prepare ourselves for God's initiative by yearning for the moment of contact and trusting that it will bring restoration when it comes. We must cultivate, as the great Anglican mystic William Law says, the "spirit of prayer" in order to receive the gift of prayer, and this involves turning our faces to the Lord in trustful expectancy (Dn 9:3). The deaf man, after all, allowed himself to be brought to Jesus, and trusted him enough to go off with him away from the multitude. But we cannot magically force God to speak. We can only await the divine voice with longing and a good faith effort to ready ourselves (through the spiritual discipline of fasting, for example) for his initiative—to make ourselves, as the fourteenth-century Walter Hilton put it, "a pure soul for the light of grace."[15]

When God speaks to us and we have prepared ourselves to listen, the ears of our hearts are opened. This is the third insight in Mark's story. Just as Jesus healed the deaf man's physical insensitivity, so God dissolves our spiritual obtuseness, helping us to hear that which earlier was beyond the parameters of our abilities. Listening involves a total availability to God in which we open the usually closed doors of our hearts to his presence. It is not a guarded listening, in which we hold back part of ourselves. Instead, it is a profligate letting-go that throws caution and reserve to the winds. It is a radical exposing of one's entire being, because it is an attentiveness that involves one's entire being. Following the example of Mary, the listening that is prayer is an unreserved opening of ourselves to the quickening of Godseed so that, as the Elizabethan poet George Herbert wrote, "God's breath" may return us to "birth."

Finally, Mark's account reminds us that a necessary condition for speaking is first learning to listen. After Jesus laid his hands on the deaf man, his "ears were opened, his tongue was released, and he spoke plainly." A child first learns to speak, as Augustine pointed out in his *Confessions,* by attending closely to the initially incomprehensible sounds his or her parents make. Analogously, we can hope to speak meaningfully about and to God only after we have learned to listen to what God has to say to us. Prayerful listening teaches us the language of the spirit through firsthand experience. In its absence, we merely mouth stale and secondhand platitudes.

Learning *how* to speak prayerfully is really a matter of learning *when* to speak—that is, of coming to a better understanding of when words are appropriate and when they're not. Too often, we presume that prayer must be larded with words in order to be effective, that more is better. This tendency is probably a residue from the urge-to-gorge's obsessive focus on quantity rather than quality. We offer up to God a verbal sacrifice purple with long-winded praise and ejaculations. But the author of Ecclesiastes underscored the hazards of such wordiness when he wrote (5:1) that "to draw near to listen is better than to offer the sacrifice of fools;" Habakkuk (2:20) echoes the sentiment when he proclaims that "the Lord is in his holy temple; let all the earth keep silence before him;" and Lamentations (3:7–9) warns us that our prayer soliloquies too often enclose us in verbal prisons.

In a similar vein, Jesus enjoined his disciples to be extremely chary of wordy prayers, for the very good reason, as we'll explore more fully later, that unnecessary verbosity tends to focus the person on his or her own voice instead of

God's. The speaking that arises from genuine listening is not an attempt to monopolize the divine/human conversation. In fact, prayerful speaking is a response that, paradoxically, is best done without words. Paul hints at this when he tells us that the holy Spirit "intercedes with us with sighs too deep for words" (Rom 8:26). Our own prayerful speaking ought to be sighs that originate deep within the heart, not endless sentences that trip from the tongue. As both the Blessed Mother and Paul (e.g., Rom 12:12; 1 Thes 3:10, 5:17) tell us, our ultimate goal is to pray constantly and unceasingly. If this is the case, it's clear that the "speaking" we do in prayer is something quite different from everyday talking.

Silence

If the heart of prayer is listening, what is it we listen to when we pray? The obvious answer, of course, is God's voice. But great care is needed here to make sense of this claim, because we fall into error if we presume that the divine voice is like an ordinary human one. It is not. The essence of God's voice is silence, and the way we attend to it is by becoming silent ourselves. As Mary tells us at Medjugorje, we must "encounter God in silence."[16] Like calls to like.

Becoming Silent. In order to listen to God's silence we must escape the din of distractions that normally deafen us to it: "Be still, and know that I am God" (Ps 46:10). There is a great temptation to let ourselves be overwhelmed by the cacophony of ideas, moods, desires, and perceptions that is our normal milieu. Sinking into the noise is so much more comfortable than striving to break through to that still point, the silent eye of the storm at the center of life's hurly-burly. The din persistently entertains us with the novelty that our senses crave, while at the same time allowing us the illusion that the richness of a life is measured in terms of how crammed it is with stimuli. But being deafened to the silence within as well as the silence without is as corrosive to God-bearing as the urge-to-gorge.

To be silent is to so empty oneself of the din of transitory distractions that one becomes fully receptive to the silence that always and everywhere underlies them. One must close the physical ears, as it were, in order to open the ears of the heart. The silence thus cultivated is not a void so much as an expectant readiness, a sensitive receptivity, to the stillness hidden in the noise of everyday life. Silence is not the same as deafness. Silence is that state of spiritual sensitivity in which the seeker makes himself available to the silence of God's voice. Deafness is the spiritual obtuseness that comes from distraction.

The fourteenth-century mystic Meister Eckhart frequently referred to this kind of expectant silence as *Gelassenheit.* The word is usually translated into English as "resignation," but this rendering fails to capture the depth of Eckhart's meaning. *Gelassenheit* more properly is that spiritual attentiveness born from the renunciation of everyday life's noisy busyness. It involves, as Eckhart says, a "decreation" of our addiction to the distractions that preoccupy us.[17] It is an emptying of self in order to create an interior vacuum capable of receiving the inrush of God's silence, a clearing of the ground so that, as Edith Stein says, we can harken

> To every stirring in the depths of...soul
> That is only perceived in deepest silence.[18]

The cultivation of the inner silence that is a necessary condition for heeding the silence of God is also frequently referred to by Eckhart as an embrace of intellectual poverty. We give up not only our appetite for the noise of everyday distractions, but also for the theoretical models and preconceptions with which we normally plug our ears. By surrendering our preset ideas about how and what the world is, we become pure listeners, capable of attending to the silent voice of God without the distorting filters of abstract (and artificial) categories.

As a youth St. Francis stripped himself bare of clothing so that he could offer himself to God in all his original nakedness. As cultivators of prayerful silence, we strip ourselves bare of the conceptual clothing that stands between us and divine silence—or, as Mary said at Medjugorje, we doff our worldly wardrobes in order to rediscover our original images. Eckhart reminds us that sometimes our embrace of intellectual poverty means we must even relinquish those comfortable theological concepts of God that get in the way of harkening to silence. In one of his most startling passages, he writes, "We pray that we may be rid of God, and taking the truth, break into eternity, where the highest angels and souls too, are like what I was in my primal existence when I wanted what I was, and when I was what I wanted."[19]

To be "quit and empty of all knowledge," as Eckhart elsewhere puts it, rid of the conceptual baggage we normally carry around with us, is a necessary condition for listening to reality—not the elaborate *interpretations* of reality churned out by our ideas and theories, but reality as it truly *is*. The intellectual self-impoverishment that leads to the cultivation of silence is the ultimate expression of humility: I acknowledge that my noisy attempts to know and speak can actually become impediments to an encounter with the divine, and I put myself into the hands of God by throwing them overboard. It is humbling to realize that what one has so long clung to as life preservers in fact are weights, and it is terrifying to jettison them and expose oneself, in all one's naked fragility, to the silent waters. But therein lies the opportunity for genuine listening and authentic prayer. The thing, as C. S. Lewis said, is to dive.

God's Silence. We are able to listen to God when we have become silent, and the voice we hear is itself silent. The divine silence is before and beyond words. Instead, it is the Word, unuttered and unutterable but always and everywhere audible to the ears of the heart. It is pregnant with a chthonic, foundational meaning that can be experienced but never adequately spoken. It is, as T. S. Eliot wrote,

> ...the unspoken word, the Word unheard,
> The Word without a word, the Word within
> The world and for the world;
> ...Against the Word the unstilled world still whirled
> About the centre of the silent Word.[20]

True, we struggle to utter the "unspoken, unheard" Word in the language of theology and philosophy or, like Eliot, in song and poetry. But these are all second-order attempts to articulate that which is essentially silent. The presumption that it can be adequately spoken violates its irreducible mystery and clothes that which is extraordinary in commonplace rags.

The cultivation of interior silence in prayer is an acquiescence to the humbling truth that God's voice is both unspoken and unspeakable. When the voice is heeded, when, like Paul, we are "caught up to the third heaven," we hear that which "cannot be told, which man may not utter" (2 Cor 12:2,4). Our intellects wish to utter what our hearts have heard, to muster up the conceptual gridworks with which we habitually categorize and tame experience. But we must finally accept their inadequacy here.

God's voice is unuttered and unutterable because that

which it communicates—God himself, the living, indwelling, creative Word—is beyond the reach of words. Words—language—seek to utter experiences, and in so doing necessarily bind the experiences to discrete definitions and syntactical patterns. Definitions by their very nature draw boundaries; they focus in on the meaning of a word by drawing our attention to what it is not. Similarly, grammar delimits the ways in which we can "properly" speak by compelling us to fit words into preestablished structural molds. But God is without limitation or boundaries. He is not simply another object in the world that can be distinguished from other objects through definition and then uttered through grammatical manipulation. God is the ground of all being, the indwelling Word that cannot be uttered because it cannot be categorized. God is mystery, and mystery is always essentially silent, unspeakable, impervious to facile human conceptualization and classification. This is why the anonymous author of the fourteenth-century mystical classic *The Cloud of Unknowing* answers his own question, "How am I to think of God himself, and what is he?" by responding "I do not know!" Through God's grace, he continues, we can "know fully about other matters, and think about them—yes, even the very works of God himself." But of God himself "no man can think."[21] The voice of nature—God's "very works"—is not the Word. The voice of the Word is silence.

Yet the divine silence speaks to us when we listen in silence. Its speaking is a nonworded interior quickening that fills us with the presence of God, radiates us with the Holy, and transforms our being through the inexhaustible and inexpressible *pneuma*. Recall that in the introduction I pointed out that the word *spirit* originally connoted an action rather than an abstract theological concept. The silent voice of God speaks by acting upon us in such a way as to transfigure the pregnant void of our own silence into a spiritual womb able to receive, bear, and birth the Word.

Word Magic

On the surface, nothing seems simpler than listening. Like vision, it's an ability most of us are born with, and our lifelong familiarity with it breeds the natural assumption that we're skilled in its use. But, in fact, we generally are not. Tuning out auditory distractions in order to concentrate on a particular sound is challenging enough, as any musician (or parent!) knows all too well. Listening in the spiritual sense—the quieting of one's own interiority and its attendant receptivity to God's silence—is even more difficult. Before we can begin to explore the silent listening that is prayer, we must first come to terms with the major obstacle to the cultivation of silence. In chapter 1 we saw that the urge-to-gorge is a deep-seated tendency that blocks fasting. Here, the fundamental impediment to prayerful listening is our bewitchment by what can be called "word magic." When we fall under the enchantment of word magic, we seal the ears of our heart against the silence within and without.

Sorcerer's Apprentices. We are intoxicated by words, particularly when they are our own. A huge amount of our waking time is spent manipulating them: we think in words, read them, listen to them, write them, and most of all speak them. They even trickle over into our slumbers: most of us dream in words on a regular basis. Our psyches are bombarded with the din of language, and we generally prefer it so. Words are seductive, and their absence makes us uncomfortable. We grow angry with ourselves if we have trouble articulating what we want to say. Irritated by others who grope for words or use them maladroitly, we impatiently finish their sentences for them or urge them to get on with it. We eagerly snatch up the latest self-improvement program for vocabulary building or speaking for success. We wish to be surrounded by words, ours or someone else's: it makes no difference, just so long as we do not have to confront silence. We are a wordy, windy, chattering race.

Words, of course, are marvelous and essential tools in their proper sphere. Human existence would be impoverished—indeed, imperiled—without them. They enable us to communicate with one another. They are the vehicles on which technical information and practical counsel ride, and they provide us with metaphors to articulate, even if only haltingly, our emotions, fears, and hopes. When spoken, words are the cement that bonds us to our fellows; when written, they link us to past and future generations. From a spiritual perspective, words—particularly when used evocatively—grope toward that ultimate reality that cannot be directly said.

But it's also the case that our word intoxication often snowballs into an addiction that has dark implications for our efforts to become listeners and Godbearers. This happens when we forget the silence from which they emerge and toward which they point, and instead presume that words are weapons with which to name and control what appears to us a feral and frightening world. They become battering rams against the silence that our verbal stupor mistakes for a threatening void. We chatter endlessly, meaninglessly, just to cloak ourselves in protective noise, and dive gratefully into the hubbub conveniently supplied by radios, stereos, books, magazines, television, and the Internet. More perniciously, as Meister Eckhart declared, we wield words in a frenetic attempt to classify, categorize, demystify, define, and hence subjugate the great enemy silence. In our clumsy hands words transmogrify into magic staffs, and we into sorcerers who wave them around to bludgeon the universe into submission.

Or so we fancy. But in fact it is words that control *us*. We are bewitched by them into supposing that all of reality is nothing more than raw material for our verbal manipulation. This delusion of power inevitably focuses us on domination as the most appropriate response to reality. Predictably, it places the self at the center of things—after all, it is I who command reality through my magical wordcraft, I who demand that the universe bend to my will through my speaking of it. What possible reason could there be for a sorcerer to humbly and expectantly listen? The world is recalcitrantly dumb until forced to reveal its secrets. The magician's role is not to harken but to control.

The rub, of course, is that when we succumb to the allure of word magic, we are not sorcerers so much as foolish apprentices who, like Grimm's fairy tale character, become the victims of our own vainglorious dreams of power. Our bewitchment by the very word magic we wield eats away at our ability to listen and hence our ability to pray, shutting us off from the possibility of an encounter with the divine silence. We are too busy speaking to take time to listen, too obsessed with manipulation to receive.

The roots of our present-day word enchantment stretch back to the beginnings of recorded history. All ancient peoples who have left written accounts of themselves, particularly the Egyptians and Babylonians, believed that words, when properly manipulated, possessed a mysterious power to bind the universe. Words of power in incantations, spells, liturgies, and curses gave their utterers the ability to control natural forces, command the will of the gods, and manipulate fate. Knowledge of how to use words of power was seen as essential for the preservation of the cosmos and the well-being of its Inhabitants, and these secrets were jealously guarded from falling into the hands of the uninitiated.

The belief that words possessed a magical power to bind reality was carried over into the Judaic and Christian traditions, in spite of the fact that both were almost unique among ancient religions in their condemnation of sorcery. In one of the creation accounts recorded in Genesis (2:18), God bestows upon Adam the right to name and thus acquire dominion over the creatures of the earth. One of the implications behind the story of Babel's tower (Gn 11:1-9) is that human knowledge of words of power had grown so great that divine sovereignty was threatened, necessitating God's self-defensive splintering of language. Moreover, Hebrew tradition had it that some words were so powerful that they could never be uttered by unsanctified tongues. The mysterious and awesome name of God could be spoken only by high priests, secluded in the temple's inner sanctum, on the day of atonement. Centuries later, in the Middle Ages, European Jews believed that the *golem,* a human figure made out of clay, could be animated by breathing into its mouth the sacred name of God.[22]

Vestiges of ancient word magic are also traceable in the early Christian Church. It is, after all, the "Word" that binds and subjugates all of creation to God (Jn 1:1-5). Acts relates the story of the sorcerer Simon Magus, who pled with the apostles to sell him their secret words of power so that he too might heal miraculously (8:18). And even St. Paul displayed a somewhat reluctant belief in word magic when he allowed that speaking in tongues was a legitimate (although somewhat idiosyncratic) way in which humans might experience and channel divine energy (1 Cor 14:20-32).

Overt belief that words can magically bind and control reality continued strong for the next one and a half millennia, right up until the scientific revolution of the sixteenth and seventeenth centuries closed the book on magic and alchemy. Most of us today no longer share the ancient conviction that words radiate a literal magical aura, even though dim echoes of such a belief are still discernible in ordinary language: we bestow a quasi-magical force to spoken or written vows, and when we "give our word," we bind ourselves to act in certain ways. But simply because we no longer consciously believe in the magic of the ancient and medieval worlds doesn't at all mean that we've grown skeptical about the power of words to name reality and thereby grant us extraordinary sovereignty over it. It's just that we no longer couch this belief in the arcane idiom of magic. More commonly today, we express it in what we take to be the more respectable language of "scientific rationality."

The sixteenth-century philosopher Francis Bacon set the stage for this modern version of word magic when he claimed that "knowledge is power." Bacon taught, and generations since have enthusiastically accepted, that the final purpose of rationality is to give humans dominion over nature. Bacon had little use for mere "theoretical" or "abstract" knowledge. All inquiry, if it was to claim legitimacy, must be instrumental, leading directly or indirectly to technological invention and control. The vehicle by which we bore into nature and wrest her secrets from her is language. To "name" natural forces through the power words of mathematics, inductive logic, and empirical analysis is to bind them in the service of humankind. The more adept sorcerers of scientific rationality become at "speaking" nature, the more pliable and subservient nature becomes. Moreover, there is nothing overtly "occult" about scientific word magic to disturb our modern sensibility. We need no longer appeal to the rigmarole of alchemical spells and incantations. Instead, we now chant the much more acceptable language of natural law and causation.

Science, then, is the modern cabbalah by which we assert our fancied right and ability to bind reality. We use its instru mentalist words of power to classify and categorize natural phenomena, and in so doing assume power over them. The more we learn, the further we extend our dominion. In principle, nothing in reality can withstand the force of our words of power. This not only reduces the universe to a tamed set of verbal or mathematical categories; it also makes us its undisputed masters. As Dael Wolfle, one-time executive officer of the American Association for the Advancement of Science revealingly put it, science is "the most powerful instrument man has known," and the society that does not celebrate and support its new class of science sorcerers and technologists is on a self-destructive course.[23]

It's true, of course, that most of us are not scientists. But the scientific spirit's overweening confidence that all reality can be classified and subdued through the language of reason has become so venerably ingrained that it percolates throughout our culture. It has bestowed widespread legitimacy on the arrogant assumption that reality is nothing more than a complex system of puzzles that human reason can discover, crack, codify, and manipulate. The driving force in all walks of life becomes a pragmatic charting and naming of phenomena in order to achieve dominion over them, and this means that our basic attitude is invasive rather than receptive. We impatiently demand that reality disclose its secrets to us, and we possess the word magic to force it to do so. Formal education, be it in the natural and social sciences or the humanities, is aimed at teaching us the instrumentalist words of power—methodologies, interpretive schemas, classificatory strategies—we need to solve problems. An individual's worth is measured by how well he or she can wield these words of power to gain mastery in the realms of medicine, finance, auto mechanics, personnel supervision, literary analysis, engineering, and so on. We no longer proclaim our expertise by donning the conical cap of the medieval sorcerer or speaking his jargon. But for all that, we still buy into a modern "rational" version of his word magic.

It comes as no surprise that a culture bewitched by instrumentalist words of power finds it difficult to take the notion of silence seriously. Silence is viewed as an obstacle to progress, scornfully dismissed as a sterile emptiness, an unproductive void that retards the onward march of word magic's campaign of world conquest, the meaningless plaything of mystics and other crackpots. The very suggestion that reality's ultimate foundation is an unuttered and unutterable silence bewilders and irritates the modern-day word sorcerer, convinced as he is that nothing falls outside the sovereignty of instrumentalist reason. Eckhart's plea for the cultivation of intellectual poverty strikes him as absurdly backward-looking.

As I suggested earlier, however, the widespread assumption that our contemporary word magic of science and reason puts us in the driver's seat is illusory. The very words of power we invoke and claim to control in fact control us. They hypnotize us with the arrogant illusion that we can conquer reality, and drive us toward ever more compulsive and blindly repetitive attempts to speak and thus subjugate it. They retard our ability to listen, and in so doing distance us farther and farther from the silence that ultimately underlies and sustains the world of natural causality. They blind by convincing us that we are masters of the universe, and that our own voices are the only ones worth attending to. They enthrall, imprisoning us within their artificial labyrinths of linguistic categories and methodologies rather than liberating us to experience reality as the God-saturated thing it truly is. For all our hubris, we are sorry magicians indeed.

Magical Prayers. Religion is not immune to the bewitchment of word magic. Just as the urge-to-gorge can stifle our ability to embrace soul-hunger, so the obsession with speaking words of power can bleed into our prayer life. But this insidious seepage is obviously fatal to that listening which is the essence of prayer. As we've already seen, word magic is too fixated on conquest and subjugation either to cultivate receptive silence or attend to divine silence. It views silence not as an invitation but as a threat to its sovereignty. Consequently, when word enchantment seeps into prayer life, the silent conversation between God and the human heart that prayer is meant to be degenerates into a noisy monologue in which the word sorcerer tries to bind God.

There are many ways in which prayer can be corrupted by word magic, but by way of illustration let's focus on two of the most common: "chatter prayer" and "genie prayer."

Chatter Prayer

The attentiveness and self-emptying that prayerful listening calls for is difficult to sustain by even the holiest of people, and most of us find ourselves, more often than we would wish, slipping into the less demanding mode of talking. There's nothing pernicious in and of itself about actually speaking words in God's presence. Sometimes prayerful talking is spiritually therapeutic, a genuinely heartfelt and humble self-exposure. At other times it may be a celebratory eruption of love and rejoicing. But when prayer becomes nothing but talk because it has degenerated into a rotely mechanical recitation of formulaic prayers, or because it is nothing more than free association disguised as piety, it is chatter prayer, a noisy, voluble, and utterly self-absorbed effort to bind God through word magic.

Chatter prayer's perversity stems from its quasi-magical assumption that one can stay right with God either through the furious verbal assault of free association, in which the sorcerer rattles on nonstop about any and everything that pops into her head, or through the scrupulous and repetitive incantation of spells/prayers. The secret is just to keep talking until one's religious word magic satisfies religious duty and pacifies God. This word magic has no need for the cultivation of silence; instead, what's essential is to keep up an acoustic onslaught of power words. Nor is there any point in listening for and to silence, because one really isn't interested in hearing God so much as in keeping on his good side by offering up verbal sacrifice.

Everyday conversational chatter is mindless, but chatter prayer is soulless as well. It neither expresses heart-yearning nor focuses on the divine. Instead, it is rote lip service whose only purpose is self-protection. It's the required premium on an insurance policy, and like most bills is paid grudgingly. Even the words the sorcerer manipulates in order to pay the bill are rarely harkened to by her; they quickly become nothing more than memorized sounds or spontaneous ejaculations. But that, after all, is the nature of magical spells. It's not important that the sorcerer understand or listen to what she says, but only that she whips through it regularly and correctly.

Genie Prayer

Chatter prayer has no other aim than to pay religious dues and keep God satisfied. But sometimes stronger magic is needed, particularly when we find ourselves in a tough spot or badly want something. Then those bewitched by word magic bring in the heavy gun of genie prayer.

The purpose of genie prayer is to incant formulae that will force God to give us what we want. God becomes a genie who can be coerced into granting our wishes if we know the words of power to bind him. The sorcerer who invokes the genie prayer is not interested in speaking to God, but only in using him, and his verbal prayer/spells allow for that. Three rosaries for three days; a formulaic plea to Our Lady of Perpetual Help recited each morning for a week; scrupulous attendance at mass each day for an entire month: there are any number of ways of coaxing the genie-God out of his bottle, and none of them involve listening. They plead, demand, whine, cajole, bribe, threaten, bargain, and conjure, and in all the ensuing racket silence is lost.

It is not, of course, petitionary prayer itself that is perverse—after all, Jesus himself taught us to ask for our daily bread—but rather its degeneration into a magical recitation of words of power. The motivation behind all magic is to empower the self by forcing the world to do one's bidding, and the magical degeneration of petitionary prayer is no exception. The sorcerer here is not interested in a silent listening to God's silence in order to discover what may be required of him. This sort of listening is, of course, the heart of petitionary prayer. Jesus in Gethsemane humbly acknowledges that in spite of his own particular desires, what's important at the end of the day is that God's will is followed (Mt 26:39; Mk 14:36; Luke 22:42). Similarly, after his blinding experience on the road to Damascus, a chastened Paul humbly asks God to give him direction (Acts 9:7). But the sorcerer knows perfectly well what he wishes and doesn't need to consult God. All he demands from his genie-God is a little help in realizing his ambitions, and he lobbies for this with word magic.

Poetic Listening, Prayerful Listening

How do we break the spell of word magic so that we can authentically attend to the silent voice of God and avoid the snares of perversions such as chatter and genie prayer? It is a poet, John Keats, who hands us an important clue. This is as it should be, because poets are acute heeders of silence. As one commentator recently put it, "poetry and prayer are cousins...both focus the mind and heart on the truths of the human heart and the mysteries of the human condition."[24] Reading a poem involves a listening to the silence between its words as much as to the actual words themselves. Composing a poem likewise entails a harkening to the silence both within and without.

Walking home from a Christmas pantomime in 1817, the twenty-two-year-old Keats was hit by a sudden flash of insight and excitedly shared it with the two friends accompanying him. The creative person, Keats told them, is characterized by the possession of a quality called "negative capability," which enables him or her to attend to "uncertainties and mysteries" without "any irritable reaching out after fact and reason."[25] The sensitive poet—Keats specifically mentioned Shakespeare as an example—doesn't impatiently strive to subjugate the cosmos by naming, classifying, and artificially demystifying it. Instead, he recognizes, with awe and gratitude, that reality is greater than any petty human attempt to control it, and that the proper response to this mysterious majesty is humble attentiveness rather than seizure and conquest. The good poet accepts the inability of language to freeze-frame the mystery in transparently logical categories and rests content with a sparing but evocative use of words to beckon to it. The words are intended as signposts, metaphors, catalysts that invite the reader to explore for him or herself the silence toward which they point. In a good poem what is left unsaid—what *must* be left unsaid—is more significant than what *is* said.

Prose, to put it another way, wordily strives to capture reality by ignoring its unutterable mystery, by irritably groping, as Keats said, for logical dissection. Poetry, sensitive to the silence that underlies fact and reason, bows before its mystery in awe and celebration. We turn to prose for data, information, and theory. But, says the poet Denise Levertov, "people turn to poems for some kind of illumination, for revelations that help them to survive, to survive in spirit, not only in body. These revelations are usually not of the unheard-of but of what lies around us unseen or forgotten."[26]

Keats's negative capability, then, is "negative" in the sense that it is a letting-go of the human urge to force all of reality into artificially lucid explanations. It is a relinquishment of word magic's incessant drive to speak, an abandonment of the fear of silence, a giving up of the demands of self. Put positively, it is a willingness to make oneself receptive to the silence within and without, to become the disciple rather than the master.

More precisely, negative capability has three characteristics that make for poetic listening: absolute attentiveness, disregard of self, and love. The first two are complementary: the more one ignores the imperious urge of the ego to conquer with words, the better one is able to attend with concentration and clarity. The seventeenth-century haiku master Matsuo Basho recognized as much when he wrote the following bit of advice for aspiring poets:

> Go to the pine if you want to learn about the pine, or to the bamboo if you want to learn about the bamboo. And in doing so, you must leave your subjective preoccupation

with yourself. Otherwise you impose yourself on the object and do not learn. Your poetry issues of its own accord when you and the object have become one—when you have plunged deep enough into the object to see something like a hidden glimmering there.[27]

For Basho, careful attending necessarily involves a forsaking of the ego as well as the intellectual filters through which it tends to name and hence dominate reality. The key is to lose oneself in one's listening long enough to achieve identity with the meaningful silence—the "hidden glimmering"—of the object of one's attention. If one can accomplish this, the object not only shines forth in a fresh, revelatory way; the depths of one's own interior silence are also plumbed. As Thomas Merton put it, attending to the "spiritual values" in the silence behind an object uncovers a "spiritual vitality" that not only discloses the object's true nature but also "lifts [the self] above itself, takes it out of itself, and makes it present to itself on a level of being that it did not know it could ever achieve."[28] The self thus transfigured is no longer concerned with carving reality into neatly organized categories. Instead, it is content to listen in silence to the silence, and this is egoless attentiveness. That's why the poet Mary Oliver insists that "to pay attention, this is our endless and proper work."[29]

Moreover, the listening born from negative capability is an act of love. The poet is not merely curious; she is enamored. She senses something in the object of her attentiveness worthy of her deepest commitment and love, something that calls her from the everydayness in which she normally sojourns by promising her a deeper meaning. This harkens back, of course, to our discussion of Sehnsucht in the previous chapter. The silence of God, the mystery that wraps around us and the universe, is occasionally intuited even in the din of everyday life, even by word magicians, and it awakens the intense longing called soul-hunger. The person, poet or otherwise, who has been purged of her addictive compulsions through the *ascesis* of fasting recognizes that her soul-hunger points to something ultimately desirable because ultimately good, and such a realization cannot but transform what initially was longing into love.

The love that fuels poetic listening, much like the love that enriches relations between humans, does not seek to manipulate, to coerce, to bind. How could genuine love seek such domination? Instead, it is content to allow the object of love simply to be, and outpours itself in adoration and service. Thus love is a reaching outwards toward the beloved and a forsaking of self. As such, it continues the cultivation of that interior silence that is a necessary condition for attending to the silence of God's voice. In the words of the poetical mystic Raissa Maritain, "...poetry thus appears to me as the fruit of a contact of the spirit with reality in itself ineffable, and with its source which is in truth God himself in the impulse of love which leads him to create images of his beauty."[30]

If poetic listening is one of the fruits of contact with the divine silence, prayerful listening is the means. The listening that is prayer, like the listening that is poetic, is not concerned with words so much as with the silence from which the words are born and toward which the words are directed. The close parallel between poetic and prayerful listening suggests that the three qualities of attentiveness, decreation (to use Eckhart's word) of self, and love that are characteristic of Keats's negative capability are also crucial to prayer. We avoid reducing prayer to word magic when we focus on God's silence instead of our own voices, refuse to be controlled by our egoistic urge to control, and open the ears of our heart in love and commitment. Thus Pseudo-Macarius tells us, in words reminiscent of Basho's advice to become one with the "hidden glimmering" of objects, that prayer ought to be a concentrated "waiting upon God, for God to come and permeate" our hearts. "Enough of groanings and sobs," he says. Listen in silent attentiveness for the "coming of God."[31] Evagrios Pontikos observes that this openness is only possible when the noisy demands of the ego have been forsaken. "In your prayer time," he says, "rid yourself of everything that harasses you"—such as the irritable reaching out for fact and reason—and become "an ignorant and simple and at the same time a pensive child."[32] And the anonymous author of *The Cloud of Unknowing* insists that it is love and not cogitation that allows for the receptivity of prayerful listening. "I beg you," he says, "to incline with all eagerness to this movement of love which is in your heart, and to follow it. Leave to one side everything that can be thought, and choose out of love that which cannot be thought. Why? Because [God] may well be loved, but not thought. By love he can be caught and held, but by thinking never....Therefore attend in humility to the unseeking movement of love in your heart."[33]

Living the Listening

Our comparison of poetic and prayerful listening clearly indicates that the cultivation of interior silence and alertness to divine silence need not be a total renunciation of words so much as word magic's obsession with words. As I pointed out when discussing chatter and genie prayer, there is nothing noxious in and of itself about speaking words in God's presence. The fault consists in focusing more on the words than on the silence from which they emerge and toward which they flow.

The Cloud of Unknowing's author similarly did not wish to discount worded prayer completely. He tells us that his cautions against verbosity are not "because I want you to stop praying vocally whenever you are so moved, or to prevent you breaking out, in your overflowing devotion of soul, in normal speech to God with some appropriate word of good, such as 'Good Jesus!,' 'Lovely Jesus!,' 'Sweet Jesus!,' and so on. No, God forbid you understand me to mean this!"[34] What he does desire, however, is to encourage in us prayerful responses that break the bondage of word magic. As we'll soon discover, it's also significant that the examples of "some appropriate word of good" he gives are short ejaculations and not lengthy encomiums.

The importance of not identifying prayer with talking, any more than we ought to identify a poem with just the actual words that comprise it, is underscored by both Mary and St. Paul. I mentioned at the beginning of this chapter that the Blessed Virgin urges us at Medjugorje to "pray, dear children, without ceasing." Paul's admonishments to "pray constantly" (1 Thes 5:17), to be "constant in prayer" (Rom 12:12), to "devote" ourselves to prayer (1 Cor 7:5), and to "continue steadfastly in prayer" (Col 4:2) are well-known watchwords of Christianity. Now obviously neither Mary nor Paul is advising us to talk ceaselessly; even if such loquacity were possible, it's not desirable. So what they must have in mind is a *living* of prayer rather than a speaking of it, the cultivation of a way of being rather than a piling up of words. As Evagrios Pontikos put it, "The excellence of prayer does not consist in its quantity but in its quality, as is shown by this word (Mt 6:7): 'In praying, do not heap up empty phrases.' "[35]

By this point it should be clear what it means to live prayerfully. If prayer is a conversation between us and God in which we silently listen to the divine silence, then to pray constantly is to live in such a way as to listen constantly. As we've seen, a necessary condition for harkening to the silent voice of God is the cultivation of interior silence, and this in turn is accomplished through attentiveness, selflessness, and love. Continuous prayer is possible when we have opened ourselves up completely to the presence of God and live that openness in our daily lives and labors. The radical response that prayer is becomes so internalized that we *live* it rather than *do* it. In the language of Handmaid spirituality, prayer is the constant awareness of the Godseed within and the desire to so attend to it with love and reverence that it increases and we decrease. It is to still one's self and lovingly open the ears of one's heart so that God's silence fills our own. It is a lived alertness—an "unceasing mindfulness of God,"[36] in the words of Diadochus of Photike—to our destinies as Godbearers. To live the listening that is prayer one must, as St. Anthony the Hermit declared, "always breathe Christ."[37]

But how to go about breathing Christ? It is not enough to have the desire to do so. A spiritual strategy or technique is also necessary. One of the earliest and abiding features of monasticism is the *horae canonicae* (canonical hours), a program of continuous prayer prescribing a number of periods during the day and night for communal prayer. But while this technique has proven fruitful for cloistered men and women (although even they must be on guard against the regularity of their prayers reducing to mechanical chatter or word magic), it is somewhat impractical for those of us who dwell in the midst of the world. Fortunately, however, a complementary strategy, discovered by the desert fathers, refined by the Eastern Church, and transmitted to the West through John Cassian, is available. It has come to be known as "hesychasm" (from *hesychia:* silence, peace, sweetness of union with God). A hesychast, as John Climacus tells us, is a person who, though engaged in the hurly-burly of everyday living, "seeks to house the incorporeal within the corporeal"[38] by making room within his or her own stilled heart for the silent presence of God. This is typically done in a series of spiritual steps that move from worded prayer to silent living prayer.

As we've seen, a constant obstacle to prayer is our obsession with distracting words. Either we seek to bind God's will through the presumptuous invocation of word magic, or we simply rattle on mindlessly and our thoughts follow our speech hither and yon. Even with the best will in the world, it is frequently difficult to focus in prayer.

John Cassian, following the hesychastic tradition, argues that the cause of our wordy confusion is quite clear: we lack a precise formula by which to recall our wandering minds and still our hearts. So in order to concentrate our attention, he advises that we focus on a short verbal phrase, ideally taken from scripture, saying it over and over, first aloud, then mentally, until its continuous repetition so calms and becomes a part of us that our hearts speak it, silently, continuously. The particular phrase Cassian recommends is taken from Psalm 70: "Haste thee, O God, to deliver me; make haste to help me, O Lord."[39] Other hesychasts have used slightly different versions. When the Abba Macarius, for example, was asked how one should pray, he replied "There is no need to lose oneself in words. It is enough to spread out the hands and to say, 'Lord, as thou wilt and as thou knowest best, have mercy.'"[40] Another desert father responded to the same question in this way: "I will show you how I do not cease praying, simply by going on with my work. I am there sitting in God's presence. And when I put my little leaves to soak and when I start to weave a rope I say, 'Have mercy on me, O God, according to thy steadfast love.'"[41]

Today the most common hesychastic expression is the so-called Jesus Prayer, usually rendered as "Lord Jesus Christ, son of the living God, have mercy on me a sinner." The actual phrase repeated by a hesychast is not as important as the purpose for using it in the first place: to keep the mind too busy to scattergun with words and concepts and thoughts of self, to train it in alertness, and to cultivate within it a silence that can make contact with the divine silence. The author of *The Cloud of Unknowing,* an advocate of the hesychastic technique, advises that any short phrase or single word will do so long as it concentrates and stills the mind. That's why, as we saw at the beginning of this section, he says that an "appropriate word of good" such as "Dear Jesus!" or "Sweet Jesus!" does not hamper but actually encourages prayerful listening.

It's important to note that the hesychasts' invocation of a simple phrase or word as a technique by which to cultivate inner silence is not a backhanded appeal to word magic. The word sorcerer seeks either to placate or to bind God with his spells/prayers and thereby augment his own power. But the hesychast has no such ambition. He does not take his uttered prayer as a formulaic word of power—witness the insistence in *The Cloud of Unknowing* that any expression will do—nor is he interested in self-aggrandizement, much less in magically manipulating God. His goal is to banish the self and invite God to fill the ensuing vacuum. His short prayer is nothing more than a means to that end.

Hesychasm, then, is a spiritual technique that takes seriously Paul's and Mary's injunction to pray ceaselessly. In reaching that still point at which the initially uttered prayer silently vibrates in one's heart, the hesychast opens herself single-mindedly to the silent presence of God. The prayerful heart-listening becomes who she is, not merely an activity reserved for periods set aside from the day's otherwise noisy activities.

One of the most gripping examples of what it means to live the listening which is prayer through the spiritual technique of hesychasm is Brother Lawrence, a seventeenth-century lay

brother of the Discalced Carmelites. Lawrence was an unedu-
cated man who entered the monastery late in life, after a
somewhat unsettled youth, and spent most of his time there,
first as a cobbler and then as a cook. But he quickly became
known as a great spiritual master, and shortly after his death
in 1691 the spiritual principles he had shared with others during his lifetime were recorded by his admirers.

Brother Lawrence referred to his spiritual discipline as
"practicing the presence of God." His description of this practice clearly indicates that it is a quiet listening to the silent
voice of God. "I do nothing else," he tells us, "but abide in
[God's] holy presence, and I do this by a simple attentiveness
and an habitual, loving turning of my eyes on him. This I
should call the actual presence of God, or to put it better, a
wordless and secret conversation between the soul and God
which no longer ends."[42]

The way to this silent and ongoing listening moves through
worded prayer to silence. Lawrence relates that he reached a
point in his spiritual development when he "abandoned all
my forms of [external] worship, and those [worded] prayers
which are not obligatory" because he discovered that "rules
or special forms of worship" can "fetter" the soul in search of
communion with God.[43] God wishes to possess and indwell
each human heart, but he cannot do this "without emptying
it of all that is not himself." In order to practice the presence
of God, then, the individual must cooperate with God in cultivating interior silence.

This self-emptying is begun by embracing Eckhart's intellectual poverty. Since the self is normally filled with the din of
its egoistic demands to interpret, classify, and control reality,
the first step toward silence is the calming of our overactive
intellects. Brother Lawrence put it this way: "Thoughts spoil
everything. All evil begins there. We must take care to set

them aside as soon as we observe them not to be necessary for the task of the moment or for our salvation, so that we can begin again our conversation with God, wherein is our only good."[44]

Brother Lawrence's purpose in advising that we set aside thoughts in practicing the presence of God is not to advocate irrationalism. As we've seen, thoughts and the words that express them are appropriate and necessary for the flourishing and indeed the very survival of humans. His point is that we too often mistakenly assume that because words are essential in everyday contexts, they must likewise be useful in our conversations with God. But in fact they are not. Such conversations, he insists over and over, must aim for "an alertness toward God," and this can only be achieved when our listening is "wordless."[45]

Still, until this wordless attentiveness has been achieved, the hesychastic appeal to short verbal expressions to focus the mind and calm its incessant activity may be helpful. The practice of God's presence, Lawrence tells us, is "somewhat difficult at the start" since the silence it entails is so foreign to our daily lives. Consequently, "it will not be inappropriate for those who undertake this practice to resort in the heart to a few words such as: 'My God, I am wholly yours'; 'God of love, I love you with all my heart'; 'Lord, fashion me according to your heart'—or such other words as love may suggest at the moment." But the words are not ends in themselves. Their only purpose it to prevent the mind's wandering and keep the heart "fastened on God alone."[46] With perseverance and trust, the worded ejaculations will eventually sink deeply into the soul, infusing it with receptive silence. It is at this point that the silence of God rushes in, and the heart can joyfully cry, "I no longer believe, I see and I experience!"[47]

Living the listening that is prayer in this way revitalizes us and becomes active, as Brother Lawrence says, "in all the processes of our life." Each task we perform, from the most mundane upwards, becomes an occasion for prayerful listening and celebration. The normal divide between our prayer life and our everyday existence is erased, and we dwell ceaselessly, continuously, in God's presence. The descriptions of Brother Lawrence left us by his contemporaries attest to the fact that he achieved this goal of constant prayer himself. As one of them states,

> Everything was the same to him, every place, every task. The good Brother found God everywhere, as much while he was repairing shoes as while he was praying with the Community. He was not eager to go into retreat, for he found in his common tasks the same God to worship as in the depths of the deserts. His whole means of approach to God was to do all for the love of him, and so he was not concerned about that which claimed his attention, provided that he did it for God. It was God, not the task, he had in view.[48]

Brother Lawrence himself said it more simply: the soul which has attained the interior silence necessary for listening to the divine silence—that has, in short, *become* prayer— "passes almost all its life in continual acts of love, worship, contrition, trust, acts of thankfulness, sacrifice, petition and all the noblest virtues."[49]

Holy Sword, Sacred Fire

The goal of Handmaid spirituality is to enable us to birth God in our souls and in the process rediscover our original image. Fasting cultivates the soil of our hearts by awakening us to the true significance of our constant hunger. Prayer waters and nurtures the Godseed by creating the silence necessary for it to blossom forth and entwine our souls.

The listening which is prayer is not easy to achieve. Headstrong and self-centered creatures that we are, we balk at and even dread the letting-go of our egos, thoughts, and words that prepares the way for silent listening. There is so much noisy distraction to throw ourselves into, so much word magic to be manipulated in our whirlwind drive for conquest, that reaching down for that still point which underlies all the thunder and lightening is a daunting task indeed. For most of us the struggle will be painful, and it will have to be renewed again and again. But the pain of the struggle cannot be avoided if one would walk the Handmaid's way. It is one of the sets of tiles necessary for the creation of a heart mosaic and must be embraced with the trust and faith that it will gradually, inevitably, make way for the contrasting tiles of fulfillment, peace, and joy.

No one knows better than Mary herself the pain and promise of so nurturing the Godseed within that one's very living becomes a prayer. Her entire life was a cultivation of the interior silence that reaches out to the silent voice of God, and that cultivation was attended by its share of hesitation, doubt, and bewilderment as well as celebration, adoration, and ultimate fulfillment. The necessity of both sets of tiles in her journey toward God is nowhere better indicated than in one of Luke's stories.

When the time came for Joseph and Mary to present their infant son at the Temple, they encountered Simeon. Luke tells us that Simeon was a "righteous and devout man" who had grown old in years awaiting the coming of the Messiah. But it had been revealed to him that he would not see death before first laying eyes on the Savior. Simeon was at the Temple the day that Joseph and Mary brought Jesus, and the moment he spied the child he knew that God's promise to him had been fulfilled. Ablaze with the spirit of the Lord, Simeon blessed the child and then spoke the following words to Mary:

> Behold, this child is set for the fall and rising
>   of many in Israel,
> and for a sign that is spoken against
> (and a sword will pierce through your own soul
>   also),
> that thoughts out of many hearts may be revealed.
> (Luke 2:34–35)

Simeon's prophesy that a sword would pierce Mary's soul has usually been interpreted as an ominous foretelling of the crucifixion. But many in the early Church discerned an additional message in it: the Christ-event was a spiritual sword that would cleave through our inmost being to reveal to us the full extent of our selfishness and spiritual sloth, the "thoughts out of many hearts." In the same swing, however, the very sword whose searing bite disclosed such painful truths about ourselves would also bring to light that marvelous, wondrous thing that lies at our very core, so deeply buried within our hearts that many of us have forgotten it: our original image, empty like the emptiness of God, silent like the Silence whence it came and to which it is destined to return. In bearing Jesus, Mary gasped at the sword that pierced her heart, a gasp born initially from pain but ultimately from joyful thanksgiving. In our own efforts at God-bearing and the transfiguration into living prayer that such a journey demands, the same sword pierces our heart and evokes identical gasps of pain and then joy.

The same point is made differently in one of the haunting tales handed down to us from the ancient desert fathers. An aged hermit renowned for his holiness was visited one day by a despairing young monk. "Holy father," the youngster asked, "what must I do to experience God?" "Make of thy life a prayer," replied the old man, "and let the flaming spirit of the Lord consume thee." But the young monk was devastated by the hermit's words, fearing as he did the agony of the flames. The old man sensed his fright and chided him. "Thinkest thou that the flame only scorches?" he asked. Then, with a tranquil smile, the ancient hermit held up his ten fingers, and it seemed to the young man that what he beheld were not fingers but ten crackling spears of flame shooting up to heaven. The old man gazed upon the monk's astonished face. "If thou wilt," he gently said, "thou canst become a living flame."[50]

So may all who follow the Handmaid's way.

Chapter Three

Conversion

*Behold, I am the handmaid of the
Lord; let it be to me according to
your word.*

Luke 1:38

*I call upon each of you to start
living the life that God wants from
you and to start doing good deeds of
love and generosity...I remain
with you on your way to conversion.*

Medjugorje
25 March 1987

*You shall love the Lord your God
with all your heart, and with all your
soul, and with all your mind. This is
the great and first commandment. And
a second is like it: You shall love your
neighbor as yourself.*

Matthew 23:37–39

Two Brothers

Deserts are desolate wastelands, but they aren't necessarily barren. Sometimes they give birth to transfigurative insights. This was never more the case than in the first centuries of Christianity, when men and women took themselves to the arid outlands of Egypt, Palestine, and Syria, sometimes singly, sometimes in community, to rediscover their original images. From that period come the various stories of the desert fathers I've recounted on several occasions in these pages. I can do no better than to open this final chapter on conversion with reference to another of them.

One day a monk came to the cell of an elder. "Abba," he said, "here is a puzzle. There are two brothers. One never leaves his room lest he be tempted. He prays incessantly and mortifies his flesh with continuous fasting. The other devotes himself to the sick. Which of the two lives a life more pleasing to God?" The elder replied: "The brother who prays and fasts in the way you describe would not be the equal of the one who looks after the sick, not even if he hanged himself by the nose!"[1]

There is a great truth in this story, one that goes to the core of both the Christian life and the Handmaid's way: fasting and prayer become idolatrous and even demonic if they do not work a transformation in the heart of the disciple that leads him or her away from self-preoccupation toward a loving concern for others. This transformation is conversion, a self-emptying in the service of God and one's fellows whereupon one's life is surrendered in love and gratitude as an oblation. Fasting and prayer prepare the way, but are not themselves sufficient. They help disclose our original image, but unless we bring love to the world in our everyday actions the spiritual insight that the first two disciplines give s risks becoming a mere abstract principle rather than a living practice. Authentic fasting and prayer draw us ever closer to the inexhaustible love God has for us, and that love fills and overflows our hearts. The essence of fasting is an embrace of soul-hunger and the heart of prayer is silent listening. But the substance of conversion is love, and genuine love inevitably seeks to act in the celebration and service of others. Because love is the culmination of spiritual growth, it always (as the desert story of the two brothers reminds us) takes precedence. John Climacus summed up the point like this: "It can happen that when we are at prayer some brothers come to see us. Then we have to choose, either to interrupt our prayer or to sadden our brother by refusing to answer him. But love is greater than prayer. Prayer is one virtue amongst others, whereas love contains them all."[2]

Handmaid spirituality teaches that what blossoms forth after the Godseed within has been quickened by prayerful listening is the Christ-spirit. That spirit is always and everywhere love. Mary's way reminds us that this love can be expressed in maternal terms. Mother-love seeks no recompense and knows no boundaries. It is willing and indeed happy to sacrifice for the beloved because it knows that the beloved is flesh of its flesh, blood of its blood. Moreover, it seeks to impart its spirit of sacrificial self-giving to others; a good mother desires that her children likewise follow the path of unconditional compassion and tenderness. Mary's own example teaches us that mother-love willingly endures suffering and pain in its fidelity to the beloved. It not only voluntarily renounces its own interests and inclinations for the sake of love, making itself a lowly handmaid in the service of God and others; it also opens itself to the risk of losing the beloved. But the promise is that the love which overflows a full heart will eventually wash away the suffering: two more contrasting sets of tiles in the heart mosaic.

In her messages to the Medjugorje visionaries, the Blessed Mother urges conversion to a life of active love. "I am calling you individually to convert," she tells the peoples of the world, "to complete conversion...to convert fully to God."[3] She emphasizes that such conversion means a living of her words, not merely a hearing of them: "Put into practice the messages that I am giving you."[4] But the only way to do that is to turn from selfishness to unconditional, disinterested love. "Decide for love, dear children," she urges.[5]

Choosing the way of love, Mary explains, involves two movements. First, we must open our hearts to God's love so that it flows into and transforms us. "Work in your hearts as you work in the fields," says the Virgin Mother. "Work and change your hearts so that the spirit of God will move into your hearts."[6] But once our interiors have been transfigured by divine love, our new inner state must bear fruit in the world. It is not enough to experience the love of Christ; we must also imitate it in our relations with others. We are called to "help others to be converted," to "give witness" by our lives even to the point of sacrificing ourselves "for the salvation of the world."[7] Mary invites us "to become carriers and witnesses of my peace to this unpeaceful world,"[8] and we do that best by reaching out to our fellows in love. There is no other way to serve God save by imitating him in his unconditional and sacrificial love. The ultimate goal of Handmaid spirituality is to give birth to the living God in one's soul, and in the process to experience rebirth as a child of God. By becoming Godbearers we bring Jesus yet again into the world to succor and save all humankind through the love—*his* love—that shines forth from us. At the end of the day, as John of the Cross tells us, what finally counts is how well you and I have loved.

This chapter explores the conversion to love that is the ultimate task of Godbearing and the final step in the construction of a heart mosaic. As we'll see, conversion involves a final turning *from* self and a turning in love *toward* God, our fellows (living as well as unborn) and creation itself. The *imitatio Christi* to which we are called as Godbearers demands from us an unconditioned love that actively works for the conversion of others to the Handmaid's way. But this *imitatio* is thwarted when we fall into the egoistic trap of assuming that love must be deserved and thereby limit the scope of our loving sacrifice. We'll explore this pitfall, as well as three ways of witnessing in and to the world a conversion to unconditioned love.

Scriptural Lessons

Few things are more obvious in both the Old and New Testaments than the primacy placed on love. Again and again scriptural authors point out that "loving-kindness" (Hebrew: *khesed;* Greek: *eleos*) is the fundamental attribute of God. The divine creative act recorded in Genesis is a manifestation of God's generously overflowing love, as is his subsequent guidance of Abraham, his liberation of the Hebrews from Egyptian bondage, and his concern for the kingdoms of Israel and Judah. Divine love reaches its fullest height in God's self-emptying in Jesus Christ; as the apostle John famously says (3:16), "God so loved the world that he gave his only Son." Scripture calls humans to imitate God's sacrificial love in their relationships with the divine as well as with their fellows. Accepting the invitation to love, in word and deed as well as thought, is the essence of conversion.

I pointed out in chapter 1 that the Old Testament understanding of conversion, or *shub,* is a turning, a retracing of one's steps, in order to return to the right path. The New Testament analogue, *metanoein,* conveys the same idea, with the explicit clarification that the turning called for is one of conscience as well as overt behavior. The Vulgate's Latin *convertere,* from which we derive "conversion," likewise means to turn around or toward. The person who experiences conversion undergoes a fundamental change in her inner state that turns her toward God and her fellow humans, and this change is reflected in her behavior in the world.

This notion of conversion as a turning or retracing is illuminating for at least two reasons. First, it is reminiscent of Mary's Medjugorje message that Godbearing is a return to one's original image, an image lost sight of through strayful wandering. To convert is to find one's way back to what one ultimately is: a God-infused being. When we convert, we return to the holy place whence we came; we abide within the precincts of the temple. Second, as the Old Testament especially makes clear, the turning we do in converting is reciprocated by a turning on God's part. When one turns to God, God responds. The embrace that emerges from conversion is genuinely reciprocal, similar to the dynamic that takes place when the prodigal son and his father throw their arms around each other.

But what has this to do with love? The turning embedded in conversion is both a turning-to and a turning-from. The convert turns his back from sin and toward righteousness. But the root of all sin is clearly recognized by both testaments as lovelessness. Therefore, when we experience conversion we turn *from* a refusal to love *toward* a surrender to the ultimate source of love. This turning, this *metanoein,* melts our hearts of stone and reawakens us to the purpose for which we were created: to love and be loved.

Proverbs (10:12) declares, for example, that "love covers all offenses," suggesting that it is through the transformative power of love that an individual is able to turn from the self-absorbed path that leads him or her away from the original image. The prophet Hosea more explicitly says the same thing when he tells his people (12:6) that a "return" to love and justice is their proper end. Hosea's inclusion of *justice* here is significant, underscoring as it does the truth that love inevitably longs for the well-being of the beloved. In the absence of this self-giving concern, what passes for love has no more substance than the morning fog or the "dew that goes early away" (6:4).

John the Baptist likewise preached against a false love that fails to birth charity and righteousness in the world. True conversion, he warned his listeners, is not a mechanical observance of religious formalisms, much less a fruitless sentimentalism. Instead, it is a genuine repentance of one's past lovelessness (Mk 1:4) that bears the concrete fruits of compassion and justice (Mk 3:8). As the Baptist said (Lk 3:11,14), anticipating the Master whose coming he heralded, "He who has two coats, let him share with him who has none; and he who has food, let him do likewise....Rob no one by violence or by false accusation, and be content with your wages." John's symbol of conversion to selfless love was baptism, a washing-away of the clay that clogs the living waters within, a going-under into the depths of one's soul and a resurfacing with the clear apprehension of one's previous transgressions and the resolve to walk a different path in the future.

Jesus' entire life and earthly ministry may be said to revolve around the primacy of love. He taught that we are cocreators of the kingdom of Heaven when we extend the circle of love to embrace all creation; thus the two great commandments transcribed by Matthew and quoted at the start of this chapter. Jesus' constant message was that true liberation is found in accepting the yoke of love (Mt 11:29), that the loving sacrifice of oneself and one's place in the world is a necessary condition for discovering true fulfillment and happiness (Mt 6:24; Lk 12:15–21), that one must love with the innocent simplicity of a child (Mk 10:15), that the daughter or son of God must learn to love as God loves all creation (Jn 13:34–35), and that we will be forgiven—that is, God will lovingly turn to us—in proportion to how well we have loved (Mt 6:12). And of course Jesus' teachings about love were epitomized by his concrete behavior: the healings, the gentleness, the forgiving embrace of the wayward, the compassionate respect for the marginalized, the innocent joy in food and laughter and companionship and nature, the final and ultimate act of self-giving at Golgotha.

Paul echoed the ancient notion of God's turning to us in reciprocity to our turning to him when he declared (Eph 5:1–2) that the Christian's goal is to imitate Christ by walking in love and sacrificing for others even as Christ loved and sacrificed for us, and that the person who so loves is "known" by God (1 Cor 8:3). Like John the Baptist, Paul also maintained that charitable actions which do not spring from an inner turning or, conversely, interior spiritual discernment which does not produce concrete acts of love, are pseudoconversions: "If I speak in the tongues of men and of angels, but have not love, I am a noisy gong or a clanging cymbal. And if I have prophetic powers, and understand all mysteries and all knowledge, and if I have all faith, so as to remove mountains, but have not love, I am nothing. If I give away all I have, and if I deliver my body to be burned, but have not love, I gain nothing" (1 Cor 13:1–3).

Short of Jesus' Sermon on the Mount (Mt 5–7) and the famous hymn to love in Paul's first letter to Corinth (13), no other text in the New Testament more eloquently testifies to the primacy of love than the first epistle of John. Without love, John writes (3:14–15), we are dead; even worse, we are murderers, because to treat others in an unloving way is to work insidiously toward the destruction of their well-being and, indeed, their very humanity (we shall explore this in more detail shortly). Echoing the good news brought by Jesus, John tells us (4:20) in no uncertain terms that it is impossible to turn toward God in love without likewise turning toward one's brothers and sisters: "If any one says, 'I love God,' and hates his brother, he is a liar; for he who does not love his brother whom he has seen, cannot love God whom he has not seen." Genuine conversion is not a matter of loving in "word or speech," but rather in "deed and in truth" (3:18). As the desert abba revealed to the young monk, prayer and fasting are nothing unless accompanied by loving sacrifice for others.

The teachings about love found in sacred scripture are unequivocal, and reinforce Mary's call for us to love unconditionally with all the compassion and scope of mother-love. If we would turn toward God we must also turn toward our fellow humans. Both movements are irrevocably linked. Our embrace must enclose all of creation, or it encloses nothing. And here, of course, is the rub, because most of us find it difficult to love unconditionally. As I suggested earlier, we tend to think that whosoever asks for our love must somehow *deserve* it. But as John tells us, the person who travels along this narrowly selective path journeys toward death instead of life abundant. Before we explore more fully the universal love which is both the source and fruit of true conversion, we must pause to reflect on "reward-love," its demonic counterpart.

Reward-Love

Just as the urge-to-gorge blocks fasting and word magic gets in the way of prayerful silence, so "reward-love" is frequently substituted for the self-giving that is the essence of conversion. Genuine love yearns to sacrifice the self in the indiscriminate service of God and humans, but reward-love inflates the ego by conditionally bestowing or withholding its favors. If the reward-lover finds my character or actions or beliefs pleasing, he rewards me with his "love." If he finds them displeasing in one way or another, he punishes me by withholding or withdrawing his "love." The ultimate litmus test for his allocation of love is the extent to which I "deserve" it, and the ultimate standard that determines desert is the degree to which he approves of me.

The astounding presumptuousness of the reward-lover lies in his self-centered conviction that he is the final arbiter of who is lovable and who is not. Of course the reward-lover rarely admits or articulates his own hubris. More commonly, he disguises it with appeals to abstract ethical principles. "It's not right that I should squander my love upon those who do nothing to earn it," he reasons. "Love is too precious a commodity to be wasted; I spread it too thinly if I bestow it upon all equally. I have a duty to love those who genuinely deserve it, and an equal duty to chasten the undeserving by withholding my love. I must not allow cheap sentimentality to get in the way of my duty." But of course all this is a rationalization that legitimates the reward-lover's use of "love" as a bludgeon to beat people into submission to his will. His true object of love is himself, and his selective allocation of love nothing more than an extension of ego. Reward-love's drive to set up self as the normative center of the universe thus displays a family resemblance to the equally imperializing motive underlying word magic, which we explored in chapter 2.

A Distasteful Example. Nowhere has the self-serving mendacity of reward-love been better illustrated than in the person of Mr. Pecksniff, one of Charles Dickens's most unforgettable characters.[9] To listen to him, Pecksniff, who lives in the pages of *Martin Chuzzlewit,* is a champion of virtue. His speech is larded with high-sounding moral discourse. Observing, for example, that favoritism is wicked, he earnestly cries: "There is [still] disinterestedness in the world I hope? We are not all arrayed in two opposite ranks; the *off*ensive and the *def*ensive. Some few there are who walk between"—and the transparent implication is that he, of course, is one of those few. Elsewhere, he rolls his eyes heavenwards and unctuously declaims that "if our inclinations are but good and open-hearted, let us gratify them boldly, though they bring upon us loss instead of profit." And when old Anthony Chuzzlewit at one point in the novel dares to call Pecksniff a hypocrite, the latter humbly turns the other cheek and meekly promises Anthony that later during his evening prayers he will be "more than usually particular in praying" for his calumniator. Everywhere Pecksniff strives to give the impression of a man who loves disinterestedly and nobly.

But in fact it is all a canting facade, as Dickens himself tells the reader by heaping sarcastic praise upon Pecksniff: "If ever a man combined within himself all the mild qualities of the lamb with a considerable touch of the dove, and not a dash of the crocodile, or the least possible suggestion of the very mildest seasoning of the serpent, that man was Mr. Pecksniff, 'the messenger of peace.' " For all his saccharine rhetoric about brotherly and sisterly love, Pecksniff is a reward-lover whose manipulation of others is horrifically destructive. He shamelessly blackmails those closest to him by threatening—under the guise, of course, of duty—to withdraw his love from them if they dare cross him. His two daughters, sanctimoniously named by him Charity and Mercy, are especially blighted by his egoistic manipulation. At the slightest sign of rebellion on their part, Pecksniff has but to raise an eyebrow or sigh in theatrical grief at their "betrayal" to pull them back into submission. He never quite comes out and tells them that his love is conditional on how well they tow the line, but he doesn't really need to. His actions speak much louder than any words possibly could.

I mentioned earlier that the author of the first Johannine epistle warned that whoever does not love is both a suicide and a murderer: his vanity and egoism are ultimately self-destructive, and the poison he radiates corrupts others as well. Such is the sad case with Pecksniff and his daughters. Under their father's influence, Mercy and Charity grow into shrewish and resentful young women who alternately cower under the lash of Pecksniff's reward-love and wield a similar whip against others whenever the opportunity arises. Raised in a loveless environment, they have no love to give others. Likewise, Pecksniff has so desiccated his interior landscape by his refusal to give himself genuinely to others that when his hypocrisy is finally unmasked and his material fortunes collapse at novel's end, he is outwardly reduced to what he has always inwardly been: "...a drunken, begging, squalid man."

The corrosiveness of reward-love, as illustrated by the unhappy example of the Pecksniffs, frequently gnaws at parent-children relationships, but it is by no means limited to them. Spouses and lovers also manipulate one another by bestowing or withholding love. On a larger scale, society teaches us to indulge in reward-love: we bestow compassion on those citizens who in our estimations deserve it, but withdraw it from those whose actions or lifestyles we deem beyond the pale: criminals, eccentrics, and, too frequently, the poor and homeless. Moreover, as we'll see shortly, God himself is not uncommonly the victim of our reward-love. We find, in short, nearly unlimited opportunities for inflating our egos through the spiritual murder of others which reward-love is. But again, as John warns us, such murder is also suicide. Let's examine this claim more closely.

The Kingdom of "Its." The key to understanding John's claim that the person who "does not love abides in death" is the phenomenon of "othering." All reward-love fragments the human family into two distinct and separate groups: "us" and "others." The us-group is comprised of those individuals whom the reward-lover judges worthy of his approval. As we've seen, this means those people who act and think in conformity with the way the reward-lover thinks they should. They deserve his love because they're projections of his own ego, and hence extend its domain. In contrast, the other-group is everyone else who, because they're different, fail to live up to his expectations and are consequently unworthy of his love. Members of the other-group of course are capable of moving into the us-group, but only if they earn that privilege by comporting themselves in ways the reward-lover deems acceptable. Built into reward-love's egoism, then, is a clannish mentality: *we* are lovable, *they*—the "others"—are not. This dynamic is clearly observable, for example, in the Pecksniff family. Mercy and Charity are so desperate to earn their father's approval and love that they adopt wholecloth his values and judgments. If Papa disapproves of someone, they perforce disapprove as well. They take their cues from the reward-lover, the clan's headsman—in this case Pecksniff—who serves as their center of gravity, and identify themselves so intensely with him that they close ranks against all outsiders.

This division of humans into us- and other-groups, into those who are "loveworthy" and those who are not, too often leads to the spiritual murder of the outsiders. In the act of "othering," we deny value and genuine personhood to those who fall outside the circle of our reward-love. They become for us mere objects in the world, with no more interiority or depth, so far as we're concerned, than inanimate objects— and objects, as everyone knows, are made to be manipulated in the service of persons (with "persons" here, of course, referring to us-group members). Members of the other-group are not worthy of closer or more sensitive scrutiny than any other object, and sink into statistical, faceless anonymity. Unlike *us*, who are complex persons walking in the path of righteousness, *they* are one-dimensional, easily definable and hence categorizable. *We* deserve respect and compassionate love because we've proven ourselves lovable. *They* persist in their unlovable ways and consequently exile themselves from the family of persons, and even when we reach out to evangelize or reform or in some other way "improve" them in order to force them to be more lovable, we do so from a vantage point of superiority and distinctivenss.

In short, when reward-love "others" persons, their humanity is denied and destroyed, and they are relegated willy-nilly to the kingdom of unlovable "its." Persons treated as "others" eventually begin to regard themselves as others, outsiders, unlovable things. Hammer into a homeless person's head day in and day out that her plight is somehow deserved because of a character flaw or moral failing on her part, and she will eventually come to believe it. Say often enough to the person of color or the gay individual or the non-Christian—or the "wrong" kind of Christian, for that matter—that she is unworthy of respect and loving-kindness, and sooner or later she will begin to see herself as she is seen. When this happens, the reward-lover and his clan of like-minded satellites will have murdered her. She may continue to be pushed along by sheer momentum, but her inner life will have been shattered.

Nor, as John reminds us, does the reward-lover escape. His way leads him to spiritual death as well. The more he reduces the world to a barren landscape inhabited primarily by "its," the less opportunity he allows himself to be touched and transformed by genuine love. He surrounds himself immediately with individuals whom he has bullied and black-mailed into "earning" his love, and more distantly with the faceless others whom he has dismissed as unworthy objects. In doing so he barricades himself against the possibility of receiving authentic love, and his already sere interior land-scape withers all the more.

The scriptural exemplar of the murderous/suicidal conse-quences of reward-love is, of course, the unhappy figure of Judas. An entire library could be filled with reflections on why Judas chose to betray the Master, but surely part of his motivation stemmed from the fact that he was a reward-lover. Judas believed Jesus worthy of his love so long as he thought this God-man to be a revolutionary who would liber-ate Palestine from the yoke of the Roman occupier. This made Jesus, in Judas's mind, a member—and, indeed, the leader—of the us-group pitted against the other-group com-prised of Romans, Greeks, and assimilated Jews. But as soon as Judas discovered that Jesus was not the person he took him for, Jesus became an "other" undeserving of respect or compassion, merely an object—an "it"—to be used.

Probably part of Judas's hope in betraying Jesus was that his crucifixion would be the spark that would ignite a nationwide revolt. Jesus thus became a tool to be manipulated in pursuit of an end. Although Judas's reduction of Jesus to an "it" did not, of course, result in Jesus' spiritual death, it obviously did lead to his physical murder by the authorities. And in withdrawing his reward-love from Jesus, Judas also felt, even if he was unable to articulate or completely grasp it, the irreparable blow he dealt his own spiritual health, and the horror of his loveless existence became too great for him to bear. His self-murder on the tree in that lonely field is a symbol of the more profound spiritual muti-lation he'd already inflicted upon himself by his refusal to love unconditionally and genuinely.

"Othering" God. We've seen that the reward-lover picks and chooses whom he will bestow his love upon and who he will exile to the outer darkness of thingness. But it must not be assumed that the reward-lover limits his egoistic judgmentalism to human beings. As the example of Judas shows, he does not. He also extends it to God.

The philosopher Friedrich Nietzsche is famous for declaring, toward the end of the nineteenth century, that "God is dead." The phrase has become hackneyed from a near-century's use, and consequently its profundity has been almost lost. It's typically understood today as a shrill cry of rebellion from an embittered atheist, but in fact it is not. Nietzsche intended it more as a dirge than a victorious hoot. When God dies, Nietzsche realized, no one wins.

What is Nietzsche trying to get across in his notorious one-liner? A better understanding of his intent can be gained from examining the context in which the passage appears. Nietzsche writes that one bright morning a "madman"—that is, a person the "sane" world looks on as an "other," an outsider, an "it"—wandered the streets, lighted lantern in hand, crying incessantly, "I seek God! I seek God!" The townspeople who heard the madman laughed at him. "Why do you seek God?" they jeeringly asked him. "Did he get lost?" "Did he lose his way like a child?" "Is he hiding? Is he afraid of us? Has he gone on a voyage, or emigrated?" Thus they yelled and mocked.

The madman endured the crowd's contempt for a time, but finally shattered his lantern on the street and shouted back. "'Whither is God?' he cried. 'I shall tell you. We *have killed him*—you and I. All of us are his murderers....God is dead. God remains dead. And we have killed him....What was holiest and most powerful of all that the world has yet owned has bled to death under our knives.' " The madman turned away from the stunned and now silent crowd, and on that same day, Nietzsche tells us, he entered "divers churches and there sang his *requiem aeternam Deo*. Led out and called to account, he is said to have replied every time, 'What are these churches now if they are not the tombs and sepulchres of God.' "[10]

When read against the backdrop of his entire parable, Nietzsche's famous epigram is much more chilling than it's usually taken to be because the line's context makes clear that it is *we*—respectable churchgoing and taxpaying people all—who are responsible for the "death" of God. And how have we "slain" Him? Through the self-absorbed and alienating poison of reward-love. We have fixed the divine mystery in the cement of our own conceptions of a genie-God (recall the discussion on word magic in chapter 2), and transformed the Sovereign of heaven and earth into a magical sprite to be called forth and utilized. The living presence of God which spontaneously inspires celebration and sacrifice is ignored, and we store away the leftover God-tool in churches or between the pages of prayer books until we have need of it. If God helps us in our moments of need, we embrace him as one of "us," and reward him with our love ("We thank and praise thee, Lord, that thou hast looked upon thy people with favor!"). If he fails to perform to our satisfaction, we wax petulant and angry and withhold our love by exiling him to the kingdom of the "other" ("What's God ever done for me? Who needs him!?"). Nietzsche's madman may be correct when he says that churches are now sepulchres. But if they are, it's because reward-loving congregants first transformed them into banks from which to withdraw magical funds from the divine account.[11]

In saying this, I do not mean to trivialize or condemn wholecloth those moments in which circumstances so crush us that we cannot help feeling betrayed by God and hence angry with him. We are, after all, but humans, and it is understandable that in our weakness we sometimes are so grieved and bewildered by the slings and arrows of fortune that we lash out at the supreme Beloved. Job, of course, is the famous scriptural example of an individual who feels he has a just case against God, and even Christ himself experienced the desolation of perceived betrayal when he screamed out from the cross that horrifying question that was both plea and accusation (Mk 15:34). Sometimes the anger we feel at God is born not from selfishness so much as genuine, albeit anguished, love: Why, O God, why do You allow Your people to suffer so?[12]

A story is told about a strange trial held at Auschwitz. A group of rabbi-inmates, shattered by the charnel house Europe had become and bewildered that the loving Protector of creation would permit such barbarism to thrive, met secretly one night as the camp slept, to try God for crimes against humanity. They painstakingly weighed the evidence throughout that long, desolate night and eventually reached a verdict. God, they concluded, was guilty as charged. Their decision is shocking but also perfectly understandable. At times humans feel they have no recourse but to rail against the supreme Parent who has the power to set things right if he but would, and if there was ever a time to do so, it was the Nazi holocaust.

But there's a sequel to the story of this eerie trial. Just as the verdict was reached, the first stirrings of dawn appeared in the east. One of the rabbis who had served as judge looked at the brightening sky and with heavy heart said to his fellow jurors: "A new day has begun. Let us now adjourn for morning prayer." Even in the midst of their horrible sense of desolate betrayal and rage, the rabbis still reached out to their God. They agreed that they had a righteous grievance against him, but for all that they did not exile him to the kingdom of things. Their love abided, even if it was now a love salted with sadness and confusion and anger.

This is not the way of the reward-lover. There is no deep bond of love between him and his God that can survive moments of tragedy or despair—or even pique. The rabbis, strong as their sense of betrayal was, nonetheless acknowledged the living mystery of the divine. The reward-lover does not. God is a "presence" only if God pleases. A "personal" relationship with Him is possible only if he acts in conformity with the way the reward-lover thinks he ought. Otherwise, God, like Santa Claus, is rejected as a useless superstition that rational adults reluctantly tolerate in others who cannot let go of their childish fantasies. He is no longer one of "us."

Given the perversity of this position, the unspoken question in Nietzsche's parable is especially pertinent. Who is the true "madman": the reward-lover, whose indifference separates him from God, or the converted lover, who even in the midst of anguish and despair perseveres in fidelity?

Turning

Godbearing is not possible unless we forsake the imperious demand of the ego to sunder the world into two parts made up of "us" and "others." True conversion, as we saw earlier in this chapter, is a *turning-from* a self that desires to possess others and God through the aggressive blackmail of reward-love, and a *turning-to* open-hearted and universal love, a love without strings or reservations. The reward-lover necessarily excommunicates those who do not please him, exiling them to the kingdom of "its." But the converted lover embraces all unconditionally, and in the process recognizes others and God as the "thous" they truly are. Reward love is always self-referential, demanding, quick to take offense and judge. But converted love, as Paul magnificently tells us (1 Cor 13:4–7), "is patient and kind; love is not jealous or boastful; it is not arrogant or rude. Love does not insist on its own way; it is not irritable or resentful; it does not rejoice at wrong, but rejoices in the right. Love bears all things, believes all things, hopes all things, endures all things."

This turning toward love, which is the heart of conversion, has two interrelated movements. First, the lover labors to bring forth the Godseed within by emptying herself of self in order to spend her energy in the service of God and his creation. In the language of Handmaid spirituality, this is the stirring of mother-love, a love of adoring sacrifice. In self-emptying, secondly, the converted lover realizes—and lives the recognition—that the same Godseed awakened in her indwells all humans: the mother recognizes the bonds between her flesh and blood and the beloved's flesh and blood. Consequently, the separateness that reward-love breeds is rejected because the converted lover recognizes herself to be one, in the mystical body of Christ, with all others. Let's explore both of these movements in turn.

Watch Chains and Combs. We've seen that the essence of reward-love is self-love, or the *philautia* (cf. chapter 1) the early Church fathers warned against. *Philautia* breeds a spirit of possessive judgementalism which divides the world into "us" and "others", with the latter relegated to the realm of unlovable objects, while the "us" enjoy membership in the loved clan only insofar as their actions and attitudes please— that is, stroke the ego—of the reward-lover. Blackmail and selectivity: these are the hallmarks of reward-love.

But converted love gives rather than takes, unreservedly embraces rather than discriminates, sacrifices rather than blackmails, and does so not out of a grudging sense of duty but out of joyful celebration of the beloved. Converted love does not see itself as reward, but rather as gift and privilege: a gift because freely bestowed without any thought of dessert or recompense, and a privilege because in flowing out in love to the beloved, the converted lover is blessed in turn. She is blessed by discovering liberation from the self-regard that habitually consumes her time and energy, and blessed also by her escape from the dismal situation of the reward-lover self-exiled to a world populated exclusively by thinglike "others" or browbeaten clansmen. As Christ taught us (Mt 10:39), it is only in surrendering the me-centered self that we discover the God-centered self. It is only in refocusing our attention from the judgmental demands of the ego to the loving service of others that we encounter the spirit within and become what we truly are: Godbearers.

If Pecksniff is the miserable archetype of reward-love, two other fictional characters, Jim and Della Young, are shining examples of converted love. These two young people are the protagonists in O. Henry's well-known story "The Gift of the Magi." Many of us first read the tale as schoolchildren, and no doubt familiarity has tended to dull its poignancy. But O. Henry's parable deserves to be reread with unjaded eyes, because it captures the spirit of that selfless love Mary asks us to cultivate in our hearts.

Jim and Della are a young married couple down on their luck. Jim's already meager income has been reduced even more by some unspecified misfortune, and the two, although not living in outright poverty, are too close for comfort to its shabby borders. But they possess two treasures in which, O. Henry tells us, they both take a mighty pride:

One was Jim's gold watch that had been his father's and his grandfather's. The other was Della's hair. Had the Queen of Sheba lived in the flat across the airshaft, Della would have let her hair hang out the window some day to dry just to depreciate Her Majesty's jewels and gifts. Had King Solomon been the janitor, with all his treasures piled up in the basement, Jim would have pulled out his watch every time he passed, just to see him pluck at his beard with envy.[13]

Now, in the midst of their hard times, Christmas is upon them, and they are without funds to give one another gifts. Della knows that Jim longs for a chain for his gold watch, and Jim knows that Della yearns for a set of tortoise shell combs for her luxuriant hair. So, unbeknownst to each other, the two sacrifice their most treasured possessions for the sake of the other. Jim sells his watch to buy Della the combs, Della sells her tresses for money to purchase the watch chain. On Christmas eve, when Jim rushes home to give Della her present, and Della frets with her close-cropped hair, hoping that Jim will find her still attractive, they discover their folly—or, rather, what the reward-lover would call folly. But O. Henry knows better:

> I have lamely related to you the uneventful chronicle of two foolish children in a flat who most unwisely sacrificed for each other the greatest treasures of their house. But in a last word to the wise of these days let it be said that of all who give gifts these two were the wisest. Of all who give and receive gifts, such as they are wisest. Everywhere they are wisest. They are the magi.[14]

To the cynical spirit of the age, this little tale is apt to come across as a corny and lightweight tearjerker. But nothing could be farther from the truth, for in fact it is a modern-day rendering of Jesus' story (Mt 13:45) about the man who gladly sold all he had to purchase the pearl of great price. Jim and Della do not simply exchange gifts out of a sense of seasonal or conjugal duty. They gladly forsake their greatest personal treasures, ones by which they tend to identify themselves, in order to bestow happiness upon each other. And in doing so, although such was not their intent, they gain for themselves the pearl of great price: selfless, joyful love. The watch chain and the combs are but the outward symbols of the true gifts they give one another.

This is the heart and soul of converted love, the desire to sell all that one has in order to *give to another* the pearl of great price. This is the essence of that self-emptying which to the reward-lover seems foolishness, and it is an *imitatio* of the Incarnation's cosmic act of self-emptying love, of Christ, "who, though he was in the form of God, did not count equality with God a thing to be grasped, but emptied himself, taking the form of a servant, being born in the likeness of men" (Phil 2:6–7). It is the fullest expression of the mother-love that continuously births God in our hearts, just as divine love birthed God in our midst two thousand years ago.

The joyful willingness of converted love to sacrifice for others flows from the lover's recognition that her "self," that incessantly demanding ego with which the world is so preoccupied, in fact is quite insignificant. For those who follow the Handmaid's way, this realization has been nurtured by the insights gleaned from the spiritual disciplines of fasting and prayer. Fasting begins the process of puncturing our self-absorption by verifying our deep-seated hunch that the only way to discover that for which we truly hunger is by refusing to cater to our egoistic urges toward immediate gratification. Prayer continues the growth away from self by disabusing us of the conceit that we can and ought to subdue reality through religious and scientific word magic. The more we cultivate interior silence, the more we heed the divine silence, and in listening to it we encounter the supreme object of love for which our hearts yearn. As we decrease, it increases; as it reveals its ultimate significance, our own inflated notions of self-worth proportionately—and properly—diminish. As our ego collapses and empties, room is made for the divine love for which we hunger, and we are "penetrated," as Cyril of Alexandria said, "by divinity, just as the red-hot iron in the fire is penetrated by the heat of the fire."[15] And when the infinite fire of God's love pours into the finite vessels of our hearts, it cannot but overflow to shower upon our sisters and brothers.

The recognition of our own insignificance puts an end to the egoistic assumptions of superiority most of us acquire through the years. It is impossible to hang onto the perniciously divisive categories of "others" and "us" once we realize that the imperious ego which posits the distinction is radically broken. The artificiality of the distinction is recognized once I see that "I" am no better than my brothers and sisters, that my "I" is no more substantial, no more privileged, no more worthy to determine who will be loved and who rejected, than theirs. The judgmental possessiveness of reward-love can no longer be maintained once I come to know my own insignificance. This is the insight behind one of the most startling of the stories handed down to us from the desert fathers. It happened that one of the monastic brothers had committed a serious sin and was expelled from the community. Whereupon good Abba Bessarion rose and followed him into the wilderness, saying "I am no better than he."[16]

We. To convert is to turn from self-love toward self-emptying, and a necessary condition for this is a lived awareness of one's own insignificance. This realization is yet another row of tiles in the construction of the heart mosaic. But as we've seen, the overall coherence of a mosaic depends upon a juxtaposition of contrasting tiles, and so the acceptance of one's own insignificance must be accompanied here by the equally profound recognition of one's great potential: the potential of growing into a Godbearer, of incarnating Christ in one's heart and behavior, of bringing forth the Godseed that indwells and gives life. As a "me," I am nothing; as a grace-filled vehicle of the divine, I am blessed.

Just as a sense of my own ultimate insignificance dissolves the boundaries between me and my fellow humans, so the realization that I hold within myself the possibility of greatness underscores the fact that all my brothers and sisters likewise possess this magnificent potential. To realize that I am a Godbearer is necessarily to see everyone else in the same light. If God deigns to indwell someone as insignificant as me, then surely he is to be found in all others as well. If I cherish the Godseed glowing within my own heart, then most manifestly I must also cherish my fellows for the sake of the Godseed that indwells them as well. In loving them, I love God; in loving God, I perforce love them. The two great commandments that Jesus taught (Mk 12:28–31) are necessarily intertwined. I cannot love God without loving my fellow humans as incarnations of that God. As Isaac of Nineveh wrote, that person is a Godbearer who "considers all human beings as good, and no created thing appears impure or defiled to him. Then he is truly pure in heart."[17] No one, absolutely no one, is beyond the pale; no one is an "other," an "it," an object. "Remember this," says John Climacus. "The thief crucified at Christ's right hand was a murderer. What a transformation in an instant!"[18]

The paradoxical sense of shared insignificance and potential greatness that conversion awakens replaces reward-love's fragmented "us/other" with the inclusive "we"—what Paul refers to as the mystical body of Christ. The converted lover recognizes along with Paul that there is neither slave nor freeman, Jew or Gentile, man or woman, you or me (Gal 3:27–28). There are only Godbearers, human beings who come from and travel toward a divine and ultimately loving source. There are no "its" in a God-saturated, incarnate universe. There are only "thous," bound together in a seamless, celebratory, and selfless love. "Blessed is he," wrote Evagrios Pontikos, "who regards every human being as God, after God...Who is separate from everyone and yet united with everyone."[19] For the converted lover, there is no "I." There is only "we." And in coming to know one's fellows as "we," the Godbearer, as St. Augustine observed, draws ever nearer to God:

> See how God will have us approach him, making us first like him that we may approach him. "Be as your Father which is in heaven, who maketh his sun to rise on the evil and on the good, and sendeth rain on the just and on the unjust." As love grows in you, working upon you and recalling you to the likeness of God, it extends even to enemies....The measure of your growth in love is the measure of your approach to the likeness; and in that measure you begin to be conscious of God.[20]

Imitatio Christi

Growing into the likeness of God through self-emptying love—or, in the idiom of Handmaid spirituality, birthing the God within—entails much more than a private scouring of one's interior. It is true that a *Theotokos* assiduously cultivates the soil of her own heart so that the Godseed embedded there can spring forth. But it's also the case that the love with which she subsequently fills must overflow—be given away—so that all may feast on the divine fruit she bears. Love entombed within one's own breast is nothing more than self-love, the disguised egoism of the reward-lover. True converted love, like the divine love of which it is an earthly emblem, seeks to spend itself in reaching out to others. After his purgative sojourn in the wilderness, Jesus returned to the world of humans in order to help them hear the good news, and he or she who would be Godbearers must do no less. We are called to imitate his love as best we're able.

There are three obvious ways in which converted love witnesses in the world, and each is founded on a reverential awareness of God's presence in our midst. The first way embraces the God-saturated natural realm; the second, our fellows, those Godbearers who surround us; and the third, the Godbearers who are yet to come.

Love for the Cosmos. In the two-thousand-year history of Christianity there have been occasional individuals who in fear and repugnance rejected the physical realm, convinced that the beauties of nature were demonic seductions that turned the mind and heart from heaven. During the sixteenth and seventeenth centuries, this distrust of nature led renaissance and early-enlightenment believers to the conviction that the proper task of the educated Christian was to subdue the "fallen" physical realm in the interests of humanity and for the greater glory of God.[21] Remnants of both attitudes can still be found among contemporary Christians, particularly in Protestant fundamentalism. But such hostility toward the created order in fact is contrary both to scripture and Christian tradition. One of the ways in which the converted love characteristic of Handmaid spirituality witnesses in the world is through a reverent and joyful celebration of the natural realm.

Largely because of the scientific ethos in which we dwell (and its consequent reliance on word magic), we tend today to think of the cosmos as just a collection of interstellar bodies whose motions are regulated by mathematically defined natural laws. But the early Church fathers, while certainly affirming the orderliness of physical creation, thought of it as something more. Invoking an ancient connotation of the word *kosmos,* they also regarded the natural realm as an "ornament" (we derive our English word *cosmetic* from this archaic meaning of *kosmos*). As Hilary of Poitiers wrote, "The sky and the air are beautiful, the earth and the sea are beautiful. By divine grace the universe was called by the Greeks 'cosmos,' meaning 'ornament.' Surely the author of all created beauty must himself be the beauty in all beauty."[22] Doubtlessly part of the ancient Church's reason for thinking of the created realm as an ornamental thing of breathtaking beauty was the common human experience of sheer delight in sun and stars, earth and ocean. But there was also scriptural warrant for such an assumption. The book of Genesis made clear the divine origin of the physical world, and God Himself called His creation "good." For the early Church fathers, anything that was good was also beautiful (Greek: *kalon*), and hence lovable. Indeed, how could the world be otherwise, since anything created through the overflowing of an absolutely loving and good God necessarily reflected his divine love and goodness. God is forever incarnational, even before the biological birth of Jesus. His presence, as Paul noted in Romans (1:20), has always been observable in the created order. "For from the greatness and beauty of created things comes a corresponding perception of their Creator" (Wis 13:5).

Put another way, the physical realm is sacramental, a visible and present sign of the divine grace and loving presence that permeates the universe. That's why natural beauty, as we saw in chapter 1, so frequently triggers intense moments of *Sehnsucht;* embedded at the material world's very core are traces of the ultimate for which we yearn. Nature, to use an expression common in the early Church, is "God's book," and to read that book with reverence and love is "to see God in all things and all things in God—to discern in and through each created reality, the divine presence that is within it and at the same time beyond it. It is to treat each thing as a sacrament...."[23] As we saw earlier, the divinely infused love that fills the prayerfully attentive heart must overflow its finite vessel, and when it does so it embraces the beauty and complexity of the natural order—God's book. To love God is to love what he has wrought. There is not, as Maximus the Confessor realized, a radical division between the natural and the supernatural, between God and his creation.

> The world is one, for the spiritual world in its totality is manifested in the totality of the perceptible world, mystically expressed in symbolic pictures [such as, for example, natural beauty] for those who have eyes to see....The operation of the two [i.e., the spiritual and perceptible worlds] is one.[24]

These gifts of physical beauty from the Beloved are cherished for the sake of the Beloved. Reward-love, on the other hand, approaches the physical realm in a characteristically self-interested way. It is manipulative, consumed by the urge-to-gorge upon nature, seeing the physical realm as merely a pantry filled with foodstuffs to be devoured at will. But the hallmark of converted love, as we've seen, is a celebratory self-emptying for and to others. When we recognize the physical realm for the God-saturated thing it is, we cannot but treat it with the respect and reverence it deserves.

At the very least, converted love for the physical realm concretely translates into actions that cooperate with rather than attempt to dominate nature. It refuses to "it" nature by regarding natural resources as only raw materials to be manipulated and then discarded when no longer serviceable. The God-bearer expresses her love for God's ornament by guarding against wasteful exploitation of it. She struggles against the pollution of the atmosphere, the oceans, and the earth, against the needless destruction of nonhuman species, and against the relentless expropriation of natural resources that impoverish ecosystems, because she is fully aware of the sacred nature of the cosmos. All creation, as Paul reminds us, groans and travails for its ultimate fulfillment in God, and the converted lover knows it is her responsibility to cooperate in this holy gestation. She accepts that task with the joy and willingness to sacrifice that is characteristic of mother-love. She gladly renounces frivolous desires whose material satisfaction entail damage to the environment for the greater good of bringing forth the God who indwells her and who is also present in nature. This may mean boycotting those commodities whose production needlessly depletes natural resources, or cutting back on thoughtless squanderings of water, fuels, and "throw-away" unrecyclables. It may mean foregoing a vacation to a wilderness area that is in grave danger of ecological collapse from the sheer weight of millions of tourists. It may even entail a renunciation of animal foods and by-products.[25] But whatever the particulars, converted love in this context means the cultivation of an attitude of loving stewardship toward nature rather than one of ecological imperialism. The world is not ours; it is not a tool, a dumb "it," whose only purpose is to serve us. It is a *kosmos,* an ornamental shimmering-forth of divine love, which the ever present God invites us to celebrate as a physical manifestation of his grace. The converted lover knows this and, along with Saint Francis, rejoices in this wondrous gift:

Be praised, my Lord, for our sister, Mother Earth,
who nourishes and watches us
while bringing forth abundant fruits with colored flowers
and herbs.[26]

Love of Christ, Love of Christs. The early Church fathers, particularly the third-century Origen, were accustomed to speak of all baptized persons as "christs" rather than "Christians." This might strike the contemporary reader as presumptuous or perhaps even blasphemous, but in fact the expression is perfectly in keeping with both Handmaid spirituality and Pauline doctrine. It is a striking reminder that we are Godbearers, called to realize and incarnate through our living the Christ-spirit that indwells us. It echoes Paul's insistence that once we do so, our egos are replaced as our spiritual centers of gravity by Christ; we relinquish our identity for his. "It is no longer I who live, but Christ who lives in me" (Gal 2:20). In fact it is precisely because Paul holds we are capable of growing into Christ and thereby becoming christs that he maintains that all believers—and, implicitly, all potential believers as well—are united together in a spiritual community wherein each member retains his or her identity but is also bound to everyone else through sharing a common Christ-spirit (Rom 12:4–5; 1 Cor 12:12–27). A Godbearer—or, as Origen would say, a "christ"—does not cease being himself. On the contrary, he discovers his true self by coming to know the intimacy of his communion with the mystical Body of Christ.

But unity with Christ, as we've already seen, also means unity with other christs. The Godbearer necessarily recognizes that the Christ-spirit he bears is identical to the Christ-spirit that indwells others, and that to love and honor God he must likewise love and honor the various members of the

Body of Christ. Their destinies are wrapped up with his; what affects them redounds upon him, and in turn is experienced by God. As Paul put it, "If one member [of the Body] suffers, all suffer together with it; if one member is honored, all rejoice together with it" (1 Cor 12:26). There is no division of "us" and "others" here. There is only "we."

The necessary unity of the community of Godbearers underscores the inseparability of the two great commandments given us by Jesus: Love God with all one's heart and one's neighbor as oneself. "The whole purpose of our Lord's commandments," wrote Maximus the Confessor, "is to rescue the spirit from chaos and hatred and lead it to love of Him and love of one's neighbor."[27] The spiritual apartheid bred by reward-love results not only in a splintering of humans from humans, but also, as we've seen, a splintering of humans from God. It also shatters the reward-lover's integrity, because his insistence on rupturing the Body through withholding love does violence to himself. The limb that separates from the body must necessarily perish. Its well-being as well as its identity is dependent upon its ongoing unity with the whole. The inevitable result of such splintering, as Maximus points out, is chaos, and chaos can only be ameliorated by the binding force of self-emptying love. As the desert father Dorotheus of Gaza observed, "This is the nature of love:...if we love God, then the nearer we draw to him in love, the more we are united with our neighbor in love."[28] When love has unified the Body, then Jesus' hope "that they may all be one; even as thou, Father, art in me and I in thee, that they also may be in us" (Jn 17:21) is fulfilled.

Mary calls upon us to strengthen the mystical Body by striving for the conversion of all humans. As Godbearers, we cooperate in the ongoing incarnation that occurs in our own lives as well as in the lives of others. Just as we cultivate the soil of our own hearts so that the Godseed may spring forth, so we serve as spiritual gardeners for others as well. As Jesus said, we are the light, the salt of the earth, and therefore have the responsibility and privilege of announcing his Kingdom and lovingly sharing his Word so that all who encounter it may become christs.

One way to spread the Word is, obviously, through the word—that is, through preaching, teaching, study, and shared prayer. But this approach is only authentic if it is comple-mented by action: a spreading of the Word by deed. We must go beyond merely announcing to our brothers and sisters the good news that they are made in God's image, that they are Godbearers and potential christs. When we meet them, we meet Christ, and should lovingly and joyfully treat them as what they are, even to the point of sacrificing ourselves for them, just as the Christ who dwells within our hearts sacri-ficed himself.

Dorothy Day, the founder of the Catholic Worker movement, was wont to quote Dostoevsky's unsettling description of true love, the love of selfless service rather than of flowery senti-mentalism, as a "harsh and dreadful thing." It is hard to offer up one's own self for the sake of others. It is a harsh duty to sur-render a life of material privilege and even luxury in order to share in the suffering of our brothers and sisters. And it is often painfully difficult to discern in society's most marginalized indi-viduals vestiges of the indwelling spirit of Christ. Yet as God-bearers we are called to practice this indiscriminately generous sort of love. Our efforts to assist in the inauguration of the Kingdom require that we make no distinctions, as the reward-lover does, when we love. As Jesus told us (Mt 25:35–45), the Christ-spirit is present in the hungry, the destitute, the mad, the broken. He shines forth from the stench of skid-row squalor, from the dazed eyes of the drunkard or addict, the devious ones of the con artist, the hate-filled ones of the racist, the hypocritical ones of a Pecksniff. The Godseed is sown in all fields, and it is the privilege of converted love to recognize and nurture it, even to the point of self-abnegation, wherever it is found. Isaac of Nineveh graphically underscores the "harsh and dreadful" requirements of such love:

> This is the sign by which to recognize those who have arrived at perfection: even if they were to throw themselves into the fire ten times a day for the sake of humanity, they would not be satisfied. This is what Moses says to God: "Now, if thou wilt, forgive their sin—and if not, blot me, I pray thee, out of thy book which thou hast written" (Ex 32:32). This is also what the blessed apostle Paul says: "I would wish that I myself were accursed and cut off from Christ for the sake of my brethren." (Rom 9:3)[29]

There are, perhaps, only a few individuals in each generation—the Dorothy Days, Mother Teresas, and Vincent de Pauls among us—capable of the love that utterly sacrifices self in order to help others recognize themselves as the christs they potentially are. But even if most of us fall short of the heights, we can certainly make a good-faith effort in our everyday lives to aim for them. We can curtail our urge-to-gorge on commodities and material wealth, recognizing that the more we acquire, the less someone else has, and we can devote our energies to ensure that the hungry are fed, the naked clothed, the homeless sheltered. Spiritual poverty—the relinquishment of the imperious ego—is a catalyst for growth into God, but material destitution is not. An existence lived on the margins, robbed of the future and tortured by an unendurable present, loses the capacity to transcend its own misery in order to embrace God. One of the many virtues of contemporary liberation theologians is their eloquent reminders of this essential biblical truth.[30]

Similarly, we can cease gorging on people, treating them as mere objects whose purpose is to service us—professionally, recreationally, sexually, and so on—and instead see them for what they truly are: fellow members of the Body of Christ, Godbearers within whom the spirit of Christ lives. We can move the Gospel from the insulated and perhaps sepulchre-like confines of our upscale churches to the streets, where it truly belongs, and minister there, as Jesus did, by example and deed. Our conventional and sometimes idolatrous veneration for the trappings of religion ought never get in the way of our call to imitate God's love. As Evagrios Pontikos so wisely tells us, "A brother had as his only possession a book of the Gospels. He sold it and spent the proceeds on food for the starving. And he added these memorable words: 'What I sold was the very book that tells me "Sell what you have and give to the poor." ' "[31]

Yet the selfless love to which the turning of conversion leads us is not exclusively harsh and dreadful. It is also a blessing and a source of great joy. Abba Agathon, one of the early desert fathers, once said "If I could meet a leper, give him my body and take his, I should be very happy."[32] This is madness to the reward-lover, but makes perfect sense to the Godbearer walking the Handmaid's way. Birthing God within one's heart, as we've seen, entails sometimes agonizing labor pains. But they are endured—and indeed welcomed—because we know they are the cracking and splitting of the divine seed that indwells us. The loving sacrifice to which we are called, the painful renunciation of self for the sake of God and our fellow humans, bring us ever closer to the rediscovery of our original image. And such a rediscovery is also a culmination, a fulfillment, the actualization of our potential as christs. The yoke laid upon us is initially burdensome to our gratification-habitu-ated egos, but grows steadily lighter. It binds only to liberate.

"Futured" Love. The mother-love characteristic of Hand-maid spirituality is life-affirming; let conversion bring "joy...in your hearts," Mary tells us at Medjugorje.[33] As chapter 1's exploration of fasting pointed out, the process of Godbearing does not demand that we spurn the pleasures that accom-pany embodiment. To do so would violate the incarnational heart of Christianity: that the material order, infused as it is with the good and beautiful presence of God, is a cause for celebration.

The joyful affirmation of life taught by Mary and expressed in the turning of converted love, reaches out, as we've just seen, to embrace all persons unconditionally as the christs they are. But it doesn't stop there. Mother-love stretches to encompass not only the child, but the child's children, and their children in turn. A love that extends only to the present generation of Godbearers remains conditional and partial. But Christ is forever: "I am with you always, to the close of the age" (Mt 28:20). Consequently, the Godbearer, in his or her participation in the loving conversion of the world, must reach out to future generations as well: to the unborn child in the womb as well as to all children as yet unconceived. It is not enough to surrender ourselves up for our fellows. We must also be willing to sacrifice ourselves for those who will follow us, because Christ lives in them too. Like us and our contemporaries, they will also carry Godseed in their hearts. Consequently, if we take seriously Mary's injunction to con-vert the world and Christ's insistence that what we do to the least of the world we do to him (Mt 25:40), we must recognize that we owe it to future generations to act in ways now that will cooperate with the spirit of their growth in God.

The first step in embracing future christs into our circle of love, obviously, is to cultivate love here, now, in the world in which we live, so that the generations to come may be born into a receptive and nurturing environment. To slightly rewrite John's famous question in his first epistle (4:20), how can I love future generations, whom I do not see, if I do not love this generation, whom I do see? This entails, minimally, that we work for social and economic justice, for a greater respect for life, and for a cleaner environment out of respect and love and compassion for our contemporaries. But we do so always—and this is the second step—with an eye to the advantages that our present cultivation of love will bring to our descendants. The soil tilled by our love now will bear even richer fruit in the harvests to come. Our efforts now to concretize love and ameliorate institutions and social practices that sow discord and needless suffering ensure that our children and grandchildren will come forth into a world where the Kingdom of God is a little more obvious, into a world in which, as Dorothy Day said, it will be a littler easier for people to be good.

The Blessed Mother bore Jesus, as we all know, in a lowly stable, a cave roughly hewn out of living rock, because there was not enough room—not enough *love* in the human heart—to provide a more generous birthing place for Love incarnate. The mother-love we are called to practice by Handmaid spirituality, the love that is "futured" as well as present, enjoins us to bend our efforts toward ensuring that the christs of generations to come will be born into more hospitable surroundings.

Mary's central message from the remote mountain village of Medjugorje has been remarkably consistent for almost twenty years: "Let your life be a testimony to holiness."[34] The path she offers us, which I have here called Handmaid spirituality, promises to crack the rind of pride and willfulness that accumulates around our hearts so that the Godseed within can blossom forth and bring us Godbearers to a discovery of who we really are. Her way teaches us to emulate the mother-love of which she is the paragon, a love that embraces pain and joy for the sake of the Beloved. That message is perhaps more relevant today than it's ever been. Mary is our midwife, our guide, our mother, and her way invites us to participate in the ongoing holy mystery of Incarnation. Truly, as the anonymous author of the fifteenth-century English carol put it,

> Mother and maiden
> Was never none but she;
> Well may such a lady
> Goddes mother be.[35]

Notes

Introduction

For patristic citations from *Die griechischen christlichen Schriftsteller der ersten drei Jahrhunderte* (Berlin: Akademie Verlag, 1897) [GCS]; *Patrologiae cursus completus: Series Graeca*, ed. Jacques-Paul Migne et al. (Paris: Garniers, 1857–66) [PG]; *Patrologiae cursus completus: Series Latina*, ed. Jacques-Paul Migne et al. (Paris: Garniers, 1844–64) [PL]; and *Sources chrétiennes*, ed. Jean Danielou et al. (Paris: Editions du Cerf, 1940–) [SC], I've generally followed the modern renderings in Olivier Clément's excellent compilation, *Sources* (Paris: Editions Stock, 1982); English edition: *The Roots of Christian Mysticism: Text and Commentary*, trans. Theodore Berkeley and Jeremy Hummerstone (London: New City, 1993). Occasionally, however, I've taken the liberty of making minor stylistic changes in Clément's translations when doing so seemed to me better to convey the meaning of the original texts. For the reader without Greek or Latin who might wish to explore more fully the writings of the church fathers in a single convenient compendium, page references to Clément are also cited, when appropriate, as RCM.

1. The names of the six children are Mirjana Dragicevic Soldo, Ivanka Ivankovic Elez, Jacov Colo, Vicka Ivankovic, Maria Pavlovic, and Ivan Gragicevic. In addition to the visionaries, two other children, called "locutionaries," have subsequently received auditory messages. They are Jelena Vasilj and Marijana Vasilj. The two girls,

who are not related, began receiving their messages in 1982 and 1983, respectively.

2. Interview with Ivanka Ivankovic Elez, quoted in Wayne Weible, *Medjugorje: The Message* (New Orleans, LA: Paraclete Press, 1989), p. 67.

3. Probably the two best-known books on Medjugorje, both runaway best-sellers, are Janice T. Connell, *The Visions of the Children: The Apparitions of the Blessed Mother at Medjugorje* (New York: St. Martin's Press, 1992) and Wayne Weible, *Medjugorje: The Message,* cited in note 2. Connell's book contains an extensive bibliography. Other books about Medjugorje worth consulting include: Joan Ashton, *People's Madonna: An Account of the Visions of Mary at Medjugorje* (San Francisco: Harper, 1992); Mary Craig, *Sparks from Heaven: The Mystery of the Madonna at Medjugorje* (Notre Dame: Ave Maria Press, 1988); Richard Foley, *Drama at Medjugorje* (San Francisco: Ignatius Press, 1992); Svetozar Kraljevic, *Apparitions of Our Lady at Medjugorje: An Historical Account with Interviews* (Quincy, IL: Franciscan Press, 1984); Armando Minuteli, *Medjugorje: A Pilgrim's Journey* (Medford, NY: Morning Star Press, 1991); Lucy Rooney and Robert Fancy, *Mary, Queen of Peace: Is the Mother of God Appearing in Medjugorje?* (Staten Island, NY: Alba House, 1985); Lucy Rooney and Robert Fancy, *Medjugorje Journal: Mary Speaks to the World* (Quincy, IL: Franciscan Press, 1988); and Sandra Zimdars-Swartz, *Encountering Mary: Visions of Mary from La Salette to Medjugorje* (New York: Avon, 1992).

4. Augustine, *Confessions,* trans. Henry Chadwick (New York: Oxford University Press, 1991), XI:14, p. 230.

5. John Macquarrie, *Paths in Spirituality,* 2nd ed. (London: SCM Press, 1992), p. 42.

6. Origen, *Homily on Genesis,* 4; GCS: vol. 6, p. 1119; RCM: p. 131.

7. Dionysius the Areopagite, *Divine Names,* III:1; PG: vol. 3, p. 680; RCM: p. 182.

8. See, for example, Eckhart's sermon "Eternal Birth," in Raymond Blakney's translation, *Meister Eckhart* (New York: Harper & Row, 1941), pp. 118–24.

9. Medjugorje messages of 24 October 1988 and 25 July 1985.

10. 25 March 1990.

11. 14 November 1985.

12. 29 November 1984.

13. 24–25 June 1986.

14. 25 December 1990.

15. 25 November 1989.

16. It is well documented that artists are frequently surprised by the directions in which their works-in-progress go. Both Charles Dickens and Fyodor Dostoevsky, for example, remarked that their characters frequently took on lives of their own and "dictated" their stories. For discussions of artistic surprise, see the excellent essays in Doris B. Wallace and Howard E. Gruber, eds., *Creative People at Work* (New York: Oxford University Press, 1989).

17. Pseudo-Macarius, *Forty-sixth Homily,* PG: vol. 34, p. 794; RCM: p. 183.

18. Sermon 11, Blakney, op. cit., p. 148.

19. Aristotle, *Nicomachean Ethics,* trans. David Ross (New York: Oxford University Press, 1986), particularly Book X; Plotinus, *Enneads,* trans. Stephen Mackenna (New York: Penguin, 1991), Book VI:9.

20. Augustine: "...to praise you is the desire of man, a little piece of your creation. You stir man to take pleasure in praising you, because you have made us for yourself, and our heart is restless until it rests in you" (*Confessions,* op. cit., I:1, p. 3). Aquinas: "All things are directed to one good as their last end. For if nothing tends to something as its end, except in so far as this is good, it follows that good, as such, is an end. Consequently, that which is the supreme good is supremely the end of all. Now there is but one supreme good, namely God....Therefore all things are directed to the highest good, namely God, as their end" (*Summa contra Gentiles,* trans. Vernon J. Bourke [Garden City, NY: Doubleday, Image Books, 1956], III.xvii.6, p. 72).

21. Benedict, *The Rule of St. Benedict* (bilingual ed.), ed. Timothy Fry, OSB, et al. (Collegeville, MN: Liturgical Press, 1980), Prologue, p. 164 [my translation].

Chapter One

1. Medjugorje message of 14 August 1989.

2. 17 April 1986.

3. 4 December 1986; 25 February 1990.

4. Ambrose, *On Elijah and Fasting,* II:2; PL: vol. 14, p. 698; RCM: p. 142.

5. Evagrios Pontikos, *Outline Teaching on Asceticism and Stillness in the Solitary Life,* in *The Philokalia,* ed. G. E. H. Palmer, Philip Sherrard, Kallistos Ware (London: Faber & Faber, 1979), vol. 1, p. 36.

6. Evagrios Pontikos, *Centuries,* IV:36, quoted in RCM, p. 131.

7. Matthew Arnold, "The Buried Life," in *Prose and Poetry,* ed. Archibald L. Bouton (Chicago: Charles Scribner's Sons, 1927), p. 454.

8. Plato, *Symposium,* 206a–212b.

9. Simone Weil, "Forms of the Implicit Love of God," in *Waiting for God,* ed. Emma Craufurd (New York: Harper & Row, 1951), p. 166.

10. Gregory of Nyssa, *Sermons on the Song of Songs,* 12; PG: vol. 44, p. 1036; RCM, p. 191.

11. Peter of Damaskos, *Twenty-four Discourses,* in *The Philokalia,* ed. G. E. H. Palmer, Philip Sherrard, Kallistos Ware (London: Faber & Faber, 1984), vol. 3, p. 228.

12. John of Damaskos, *On Virtues and Vices,* PG: vol. 95, p. 88; RCM: p. 135.

13. Although Dostoevsky was not an enemy of institutionalized Christianity, he had a typically slavophile's wariness of Roman Catholicism, and probably is taking a shot at it in his parable.

14. "Cheap grace means grace as a doctrine, a principle, a system. It means forgiveness of sins proclaimed as a general truth, the love of God taught as the Christian 'conception.' An intellectual assent to that idea is held to be of itself sufficient to secure remission of sins. The Church which holds the correct doctrine of grace has, it is supposed, *ipso facto* a part of that grace. In such a Church the world finds a cheap covering for its sins; no contrition is required, still less any real desire to be delivered from sin. Cheap grace therefore amounts to a denial of the living Word...." Dietrich Bonhoeffer, *The Cost of Discipleship* (New York: Collier, 1963), pp. 45–46.

15. Wallace Stevens, "Notes Toward a Supreme Fiction," "The Bird with the Coppery, Keen Claws," and "An Ordinary Evening in New Haven," in *The Palm at the End of the Mind and Other Poems,* ed. Holly Stevens (New York: Vintage, 1972), pp. 226–27, 57, 337. Stevens's attitude towards Christianity is complicated; for

a good recent study, consult Charles M. Murphy, *Wallace Stevens: A Spiritual Poet in a Secular Age* (Mahwah, NJ: Paulist, 1997).

16. C. S. Lewis, "The Weight of Glory," in *The Weight of Glory and Other Addresses* (New York: Collier, 1980), pp. 3–4.

17. See especially Kierkegaard's treatment in "Diary of the Seducer," *Either/Or*, trans. David F. Swenson and Lillian Marvin Swenson (Princeton: Princeton University Press, 1971), pp. 297–440.

18. "The Weight of Glory," op. cit., p. 7.

19. Athanasius, *On Virginity*, 6; PG: vol. 28, p. 260; RCM: p. 141.

20. Peter of Damaskos, *A Treasury of Divine Knowledge*, XI, in *The Philokalia*, op. cit., vol. 3, p. 112.

21. Peter of Damaskos, VIII, ibid., p. 231.

22. See especially chaps. 1 and 2 of *Nicomachean Ethics*, op. cit.

23. Diadochus of Photike, *Gnostic Chapters*, 44; SC: vol. 5, p. 111; RCM: p. 140.

24. This scene is not in the original play, but as a rule the BBC version follows Nicholson's original script rather closely. William Nicolson, *Shadowlands* (New York: Plume, 1991).

25. Athanasius, *On Virginity*, 8; PG: vol. 28, p. 261; RCM: p. 142.

26. Diadochus of Photike, *Gnostic Chapters*, 45; SC: vol. 5, p. 111; RCM: p. 143.

27. Alfred Tennyson, "The Lotus Eaters," in *Poetical Works* (Chicago: Belford, Clarke, 1901), p. 47.

Chapter Two

1. For example, Medjugorje messages of 19 April 1984; 24 May 1984; 21 July 1984; 15 November 1984; 28 March 1985.

2. 15 October 1986.

3. 17 January 1984.

4. 16 May 1985.

5. 2 May 1985.

6. 20 March 1986.

7. 25 August 1987.

8. 25 August 1989.

9. 3 August 1986.

10. 14 September 1986.

11. 24 April 1986.

12. Evagrios Pontikos, *On the Eight Spirits of Evil,* 1; PG: vol. 79, p. 1145; RCM: p. 142.

13. 18 December 1990.

14. 25 October 1990.

15. Walter Hilton, *The Scale of Perfection,* trans. John P. H. Clark and Rosemary Dorward (Mahwah, NJ: Paulist Press, 1991), II:46, p. 301.

16. 25 July 1989.

17. See, for example, Sermons 15 ("Into the Godhead"), 24

("God Enters a Free Soul"), and 28 ("Blessed Are the Poor") in Blakney, op. cit., pp. 165-69, 207-11, 227-31.

18. Edith Stein, "I Am Always in Your Midst," in *The Hidden Life: Collected Works of Edith Stein,* ed. L. Gelber and Michael Linssen (Washington, DC: ICS Publications, 1992), p. 117.

19. Meister Eckhart, Sermon 28 ("Blessed Are the Poor"), in Blakney, op. cit., p. 231.

20. T. S. Eliot, "Ash Wednesday," in *The Complete Poems and Plays, 1909-1950* (New York: Harcourt, Brace & World, 1952), p. 65.

21. *The Cloud of Unknowing,* trans. Clifton Wolters (Middlesex: Penguin, 1961), chap. 6, p. 59.

22. For a classic treatment of word magic, see Lynn Thorndike, A *History of Magic and Experimental Science* (New York: Macmillan, 1923), especially vol. 1.

23. Dael Wolfle, "Science and Public Understanding," in *The New Scientist: Essays on the Methods and Values of Modern Science,* ed. Paul C. Obler and Herman A. Estrin (New York: Anchor, 1962), p. 126.

24. Gregory Wolfe, "Sketching the Image: Finding a Place for Religious Humanism," *Prism* 4 (July/August 1997): p. 13.

25. Keats first described his discovery of negative capability in a letter to his brothers George and Thomas, dated 21 December 1817. See *The Selected Letters of John Keats,* ed. Lionel Trilling (Garden City, NY: Doubleday, 1956), pp. 102-04.

26. Denise Levertov, *New and Selected Essays* (New York: New Directions, 1992), p. 150.

27. Matsuo Basho, *The Narrow Road to the Deep North and*

Other Travel Sketches, trans. Nobuyuki Yuasa (New York: Penguin, 1983), p. 33.

28. Thomas Merton, *No Man Is an Island* (New York: Harcourt Brace Jovanovich, 1983), p. 34.

29. Mary Oliver, *White Pine: Poems and Prose Poems* (New York: Harcourt Brace, 1994), p. 8.

30. Raissa Maritain, *Raissa's Journal* (New York: Magi Books, 1974), p. 374.

31. Pseudo–Macarius, *Homilies,* 33; PG: vol. 34, p. 741; RCM: pp. 184–85.

32. Evagrios Pontikos, *Parenticus,* quoted in RCM, p. 185.

33. *The Cloud of Unknowing,* op. cit., chap. 6, p. 60.

34. Ibid., chap. 48, p. 109.

35. Evagrios Pontikos, *On Prayer,* in *The Philokalia,* op. cit., vol. 1, p. 71.

36. Diadochus of Photike, *Gnostic Chapters,* 56; SC: vol. 5, p. 117; RCM: 204.

37. Athanasius, *Life of Anthony,* trans. Robert C. Gregg (Mahwah, NJ: Paulist Press, 1980), p. 97. I've slightly modified Gregg's rendering.

38. John Climacus, *The Ladder of Divine Ascent,* 27th Step, quoted in RCM, p. 202.

39. John Cassian, *Conferences,* in *Nicene and Post-Nicene Fathers,* ed. Philip Schaff and Henry Wace (Peabody, MA: Hendrickson, 1994), vol. 11, p. 405.

40. *Sayings of the Desert Fathers,* Macarius, 19; PG: vol. 65, p. 269; RCM: p. 203.

41. Ibid., Lucius; PG: vol. 65, p. 253; RCM: 203.

42. Brother Lawrence, *The Practice of the Presence of God,* trans. E. M. Blaiklock (Nashville, TN: Thomas Nelson, 1982), p. 44.

43. Ibid.

44. Ibid., p. 24.

45. Ibid., p. 73.

46. Ibid., p. 76.

47. Ibid., p. 77.

48. Ibid., p. 88.

49. Ibid., p. 77.

50. *The Desert Fathers,* trans. Helen Waddell (Ann Arbor, MI: University of Michigan Press, 1957), p.112.

Chapter Three

1. *The Desert Fathers,* trans. Helen Waddell (Ann Arbor, MI: University of Michigan Press, 1957), p.124.

2. John Climacus, *The Ladder of Ascent,* 26th Step, quoted in RCM, p. 279.

3. Medjugorje messages of 13 February 1986 and 25 January 1988.

4. 25 August 1990.

5. 20 November 1986.

6. 25 April 1985.

7. 30 January 1986; 25 February 1988.

8. 25 July 1990.

9. A more complex and haunting literary example of reward-love is Shakespeare's unhappy King Lear, rich in years but poor in wisdom. At the beginning of the play, Lear proposes to divide his kingdom among his daughters in proportion to the extent they swear their love and loyalty to him. Goneril and Regan eagerly and duplicitously give Lear the verbal homage he demands, but Cordelia remains silent, refusing to allow her love to be purchased. Lear thereupon rewards his two dishonest daughters and disinherits the honest one, thereby setting the stage for his own destruction.

10. Friedrich Nietzsche, *The Gay Science,* trans. Walter Kaufmann (New York: Vintage, 1974), paragraph 125.

11. The other great existentialist thinker of the nineteenth century, Søren Kierkegaard (1813–55) would have heartily agreed with this sentiment. Although as fervent a Christian as Nietzsche was an atheist, Kierkegaard concurred that institutional Christianity had gone a long way toward destroying the spirit of Christ's message. See especially his *Attack upon Christendom,* trans. Walter Lowrie (Princeton: Princeton University Press, 1968) and *Practice in Christianity,* trans. Howard V. and Edna H. Hong (Princeton: Princeton University Press, 1991).

12. For an interesting recent treatment, see Katharine Dell, *Shaking a Fist at God: Struggling with the Mystery of Undeserved Suffering* (Liguouri, MO: Triumph Books, 1995).

13. O. Henry, "The Gift of the Magi," in *Short Stories* (New York: Lancer Books, 1968) pp. 20–21.

14. Ibid., p. 27.

Notes

15. Quoted in Vladimir Lossky, *The Vision of God* (Crestwood, NY: St. Vladimir's Seminary Press, 1983), p. 98.

16. *The Sayings of the Desert Fathers,* trans. Benedicta Ward SLG (London: A.R. Mowbray, 1975), p.35. Another story of similar intensity comes to us from the desert. One day Abba Moses was summoned to a trial of one of his brothers who had been accused of wrongdoing. Moses carefully filled a large bag with sand, pricked a hole in the bottom of it, and slung the heavy bag over his shoulder. Then he set out walking to the building where the brother's trial was to be held. Monks he encountered along the way noticed the trail of sand, and when they asked Moses what he was about he replied: "What you see are my sins, following me wherever I go." *The Desert Fathers,* trans. Helen Waddell (Ann Arbor, MI: University of Michigan Press, 1957), p. 96.

17. Isaac of Ninevah, *Ascetic Treatises,* 85, quoted in RCM, p. 283.

18. John Climacus, *The Ladder of Divine Ascent,* 10th Step, quoted in RCM, p. 282.

19. Evagrios Pontikos, *On Prayer,* in *The Philokalia,* op. cit., vol. 1, p. 68.

20. Quoted in John Burnaby, *Amor Dei: A Study of the Religion of St. Augustine* (London: Hodder & Stoughton, 1938), pp. 81–82.

21. A now classic study of Renaissance and Enlightenment Christian attitudes toward nature can be found in Carolyn Merchant, *The Death of Nature: Women, Ecology, and the Scientific Revolution* (San Francisco: Harper & Row, 1980).

22. Hilary of Poitiers, *On the Trinity,* I:7, in *Nicene and Post-Nicene Fathers,* op. cit., vol. 9, p. 42.

23. Kallistos Ware, "Ways of Prayer and Contemplation," in

Christian Spirituality: Origins to the Twelfth Century, ed. Bernard McGinn and John Meyendorff (New York: Crossroad, 1985), p. 398.

24. Maximus the Confessor, *Mystagogia,* 2; PG: vol. 91, p. 669; RCM: p. 219.

25. For a masterful discussion of Christian vegetarianism, see Andrew Linzey, *Animal Rights: A Christian Assessment of Man's Treatment of Animals* (London: SCM Press, 1976).

26. St. Francis, "The Canticle of Brother Sun," quoted in Lawrence Cunningham and Dennis Stock, *Saint Francis of Assisi* (San Francisco: Harper & Row, 1981), p. 11. The German philosopher and one-time Jesuit seminarian Martin Heidegger has written with sensitivity and insight on a reverential and celebratory embrace of nature. See especially his essay "The Question Concerning Technology," in *Basic Writings,* ed. David Farrell Krell (San Francisco: Harper, 1993).

27. Maximus the Confessor, *Centuries on Charity,* IV; PG: vol. 90, p. 1061; RCM, p. 277.

28. Dorotheus of Gaza, *Instructions;* SC: vol. 92, p. 286; RCM: p. 272.

29. Isaac of Ninevah, *Ascetic Treatises,* 81, quoted in RCM, p. 275.

30. It's instructive to keep in mind these beautiful words of Gregory of Nyssa (*On Love of the Poor,* 1; PG: vol. 46, p. 247; RCM, p. 296): "Do not despise the poor. Ask yourself who they are and you will discover their greatness. They have the face of our Savior...the poor are the stewards of our hope, the guardians of the Kingdom. It is they who open the door to the righteous, and close it to the wicked and self-centered."

31. Evagrios Pontikos, *Practicus,* 97; SC: vol. 171, p. 704; RCM, p. 280.

32. Quoted in *RCM,* p. 280.

33. Medjugorje message, 25 June 1990.

34. 25 April 1988.

35. Anonymous, "I sing of a maiden," in *The New Oxford Book of Christian Verse,* ed. Donald Davie (Oxford: Oxford University Press, 1988), p. 21.